Reminiscences and Reflexions of a Mid and Late Victorian by Ernest Belfort Bax
Prism Key Press | www.prismkeypress.com

ISBN: 978-1463690472

# Reminiscences and Reflexions of a Mid and Late Victorian

Ernest Belfort Bax

# Contents

# Preface

The following chapters were written at intervals during the year 1916. They were taken in hand on the suggestion of two well-known London publishers, who assured me that autobiographical notes, reminiscences, and reflexions were, barring fiction and travels, the form of literature in which the British public showed most interest at the present time. One's natural modesty, assuming one to be a mentally fairly well-conducted person, makes one more or less diffident in writing about oneself. Whether I answer to the above description or not, certain it is that in penning these pages I have felt a shyness in recording personal facts, which has led me to damp down the personal note as a general rule throughout the book – some friendly critics, to whom I have shown a portion of the manuscript, say too much so. Be this as it may, the aim I have kept before me in writing these somewhat disjointed notes and reminiscences has been rather to offer data and suggestions, slight and scattered though they may be, for the due appreciation, now or hereafter, of the particular period of historic time in which my life has been cast – to wit, roughly speaking, the last third of the nineteenth and the opening years of the twentieth century.

For the rest, I am well aware that the present class of work affords ample scope for the detractors animadversions of the anonymous critic who wants to be "nasty." In a work of reminiscences and reflexions there are almost bound to be some reminiscences which strike some reader or other as being uninteresting and perhaps trivial. These may be the very parts of the book which attract another class of reader. Of the reflexions, again, naturally, while some will appeal to one, the same will antagonize another reader.

As regards reviewers, in this connexion, I suppose I shall come off badly at the hands of him or her whose views are those of pro-Feminist fanaticism, who will doubtless find the book very insipid, or at least will say so. The religious fanatic who has the charge of noticing the book in the Press will also probably have his "knife into me," and express himself to a similar scornful effect. These are things of course an author has to put up with in taking up a definite standpoint on controversial subjects where feeling runs high.

Notwithstanding such not unbiased judgments that I probably have to expect from the aforesaid reviewers, I must plead guilty to the conviction that there are those among the reading public who, should they come across the book, will find at least something to interest them in the somewhat varied contents of its pages.

PS.-The publication of this book has been unavoidably delayed for more than a year, mainly owing to the difficulties attending the operations of the printing and publishing trades at the present time. Meanwhile, I may remark, the death of more than one person alluded to in the following pages as living has unhappily supervened. Since 1916 changes, moreover, in the political situation, notably the Russian Revolution and its developments, have taken place. These events, however, I do not think materially affect anything in the contents of the volume.

*E.B.B*
*January 26, 1918*

# I. Reminiscences of Childhood and Youth

AMONG the crowd of vaguely remembered trivial incidents of very early childhood, the earliest that has distinctly impressed itself upon my mind is the identification of the colour blue in general with the sky in particular. This I have reason to believe occurred at Leamington about the month of September in the year 1857. I must have been then a little over three years of age, having been born on July 23, 1854. One or two other things I can recall concerning childish ways of regarding the world which illustrate the parallel between the mind of the young child and that of primitive man. I can recall, for instance, how on one occasion our cat returned to the kitchen one morning with evidences of having been out in a fight during the night. How well I remember, in pondering over the incident of the battle of the cats, that I could not divest myself of the notion of their having talked to each other and so started the quarrel, although well aware that my elders did not believe in animals talking. Mine was then clearly a state of mind in which myths of talking beasts arise in early ages. It is undoubtedly an interesting fact to be able to recollect, if only in a glimpse or two, a childish mental condition, quickly outgrown, but which indicates having passed through a state of mind, however transitory, corresponding to that of primitive humanity.

The scene of most of my earlier childish reminiscences was Brighton, where we lived for some years. At that time the atmosphere of the George IV period still lingered in the town. Superannuated old gentlemen, in costume approaching that of the earlier part of the century, were still occasionally to be seen sunning themselves on the sea-front, and especially in the Kings Road, of an afternoon. It was at Brighton that I first became aware of the larger issues of the world. The American Civil War and the cotton famine in Lancashire were among my earliest recollections of public events. The International Exhibition of

1862, to which I was taken late the following Autumn, was also a noteworthy event of the time to me. I remember the talk occasioned by Encke's comet in 1861, but as it was in the middle of Summer I was never allowed to stop up late enough to see it myself.

At that time yellow-bodied carriages with a mottled black and white dog running behind them were still to be seen rolling up and down the King's Road. Then was the period – that of the early sixties – of the universal pot-hat (the old beaver was still occasionally to be seen with elderly gentlemen), of the broadcloth frock coat, of women with enormous crinolines – the younger ones with hair done up in nets, the older ones sporting long curls ; of tallow candles, which might be seen hanging up in bundles outside oil-shops, of bedroom candlesticks with their necessary snuffers. Gas had only recently been introduced into private houses and was still looked at askance by some as a dangerous innovation. The tea-urn was in its afternoon glory. Daguerreotype photographs were by no means out of date, though they were just beginning to be superseded by the more modern photography. Smoking was not as yet very common among the middle classes, but where practised, it was chiefly in the form of the cigar, cigarettes being quite unknown to the general public. Dickens, it may be remembered, in **Nicholas Nickleby**, describes it as a distinguishing mark of some Spaniards he alludes to, that they smoked what he calls "little paper cigars." The clay pipe was universal among the working classes.

Turning to the literature of the period, in the department of fiction the great lights of the early sixties were of course Thackeray who died in 1863, Dickens, Wilkie Collins, Bulwer Lytton, and a host of minor writers, such as Anthony Trollope, Whyte Melville, Mrs. Henry Wood, Miss Braddon, etc., who produced novels sold in red and yellow covers which were prominent in all station bookstalls. For the more intellectual reader the works of the Brontes, George Eliot, and Charles Kingsley were the vogue. In the more serious departments,

10

Hallam and Macaulay, recently dead, Carlyle, Mill, Grote, etc., were in the heyday of their glory as embodying the cultured side of English life. Poetry was represented chiefly by Longfellow and Tennyson. Browning's fame came a little later. Darwin had but recently startled the public and shocked the theological world by the publication of the **Origin of Species**. But the really cultured class existing at that time in England was, as compared with the present generation, a very restricted one. The intellectual possibilities of the English people were then stunted and cramped by the influence of the dogmatic Calvinistic theology which was the basis of its traditional religious sentiment.

The life our family lived during my childhood was, owing to various causes, exceptionally quiet and retired. Most of the relations and friends who used to visit us were socially uninteresting and of no great account from the side of intellectually profitable intercourse. My paternal grandfather, I may mention, however, whose family originally came from Ockley, in Surrey, was born in the year 1777, dying in 1868, and was consequently in a position to remember the French Revolution. I recollect as a child once questioning him upon the subject, and his relating to me the horrible reports of civil slaughter in Paris that reached his native village. I have since thought that the special event he may have had in his mind was possibly the September massacres of 1792. But the old man, to my disappointment, showed a tendency to switch his conversation off on to the more recent events of 1848, which seemed to me a very insipid change of venue. My grandfather also recollected hearing some of the great singers of the early part of the nineteenth century, notably John Braham. On the whole, however, as will be seen, it was my lot to grow up under no very favourable conditions for intellectual development. The subjects talked of in the family circle were mainly connected with religious dogma, or the sectarian interests of the various religious bodies. Preachers and the pure quality of their orthodoxy, as opposed on the one side to "Romanism" and on the other to

"Latitudinarianism," bulked largely among the topics of conversation with ours as with other middle-class families at the time. A severe censorship in the matter of the literature that was allowed into the house was maintained. The only reading encouraged was that directly or indirectly favouring the "Evangelical" theology. As usual with the bulk of early and mid-Victorian middle-class society, the theatre in all its forms was banned. In fact in many cases, ours among them, any form of amusement was supposed to savour more or less of godlessness. In those where it was not absolutely forbidden there was a tinge of disapproval attaching to it as having the shadow of "worldliness" upon it.

The most cruel of all the results of mid-Victorian religion was perhaps the rigid enforcement of the most drastic Sabbatarianism. The horror of the tedium of Sunday infected more or less the whole of the latter portion of the week. Many a story was laid before the youth of the period to the effect that the boy who began by Sabbath-breaking inevitably ended his days on the gallows. In fact, didactic narrative, often embodied in the form of the religious tract, was a much commended means in the Evangelical world for converting the sinner from the error of his ways. Thus, to discourage the gratification of the taste for the drama, a moral, inculcating the retribution which the Evangelical God sometimes inflicted on frequenters of "play-houses," was drawn from the history of fires that had taken place in theatres. But this was not all – I can recall a tract (I think it was) which told the story of the conversion of a lady playgoer who, on passing into the theatre, was struck by seeing the words "To the pit" in illuminated letters in front of her. The notion that entering the pit of a theatre would inevitably land her ultimately in the other "pit" said to be bottomless, appealed to her as a solemn warning; so she turned back, sought out a suitable conventicle, and became a converted character.

But although brought up in this hot-bed of Calvinistic Methodism, and hearing the duties of becoming converted and of cultivating one's soul in the directions approved of by the Evangelical sects, the whole theological business never affected me very deeply. The introspection of the soul and the whole sentiment connected with the Christian cult did not specially appeal to me. I believed in it, of course, in a way, knowing nothing else, and hence it being the only theory of the universe available for my young intelligence. What interested me more than any maunderings anent the individual soul, being "born again" and the like, was when my old governess, who took a truly maternal interest in me, used to talk to me about Daniel's image and its four monarchies. This gave me, in its way and within the limits of the current orthodox creed, a theory of history, such as it was, and I have always felt the need of an intelligible doctrine of history. It appeared to me as much more interesting than any reflexions on the communion of the individual soul with the living presence of its God or its Saviour, and so forth. But if my childish belief in Christian dogmas was somewhat perfunctory, there was one thing that I did believe in, although I did not talk much about it, and that was the supernatural. The somewhat inconsequent assurances of my elders that God, although in the past He had done so, did not permit any manifestation of the supernatural since the beginning of the Christian era, and certainly not in our days, was not quite good enough for me. The credentials of their assurances in this connexion seemed to rue doubtful, and the assurance itself to express a purely arbitrary assumption.

The foregoing were the current ideas of the English middle class half a century ago. In economics and politics a few crude aphorisms were supposed sufficient to satisfy every reasonable mind. The economic problem of the distribution of wealth, of the antithesis of rich and poor, was supposed to be satisfactorily accounted for and settled by the assumption that wealth was the reward of industry and virtue, and poverty the result of laziness and incompetence, either in the present generation or their fathers. The politics of the middle classes of

13

the sixties was Manchester School Liberalism, coloured more or less-more in some circles and with some persons, less in others – with a snobbish deference to the upper classes, and especially Queen Victoria, who, the middle-class mind of the time flattered itself, was a woman after its own heart. Cobden, Bright, and Palmerston were names to conjure with in middle-class political circles. As regards foreign politics, the views of the English middle classes were largely dictated by their anti-Catholic sentiments, Garibaldi was their popular hero, for example, even more because he fought against the Papal domination in Italy than as a national patriot. This feeling played a part with many people even as late as 1870 in determining the strong sympathy with Germany in the Franco-Prussian War of that year. In short, the middle-class mind of fifty and sixty years ago ran in certain well-defined grooves which determined its attitude in all particular cases. The main interest, for the middle-class man or woman of the period in question, outside "business" or the "home" was, as already intimated, religion, especially the internecine rivalry and quarrels of the various Christian sects and churches. For art there was little feeling. In fact, there is only one form of art which can be specially associated with the society of the period, and that was in music, viz. the Oratorio. It is true even the Oratorio, as being a form of public entertainment, was looked upon somewhat doubtfully by the ultra pious. But still Oratorio music did undoubtedly represent the special form in which the consciousness of the society in question seemed to find its artistic expression. For every society has its own artistic expression, such as it is and what there is of it. That the intrinsically ugly and, to many of us to-day, repulsive Calvinistic theology of Evangelicalism could have given birth to any genuine feeling at all, it is difficult to understand. But, as I said above, such as it was, undoubtedly it received its expression in the Oratorio music of Handel and Mendelssohn, particularly in the *Messiah* and the *Elijah*. I would signalize especially, in this respect, as typical, the aria *O Rest in the Lord*. It is said that when Mendelssohn had written this melody he was inclined to strike it out of his work as

14

being too sickly sweet, but was prevailed upon by his friends to leave it in. That the composer was intrinsically right in his estimate of it will be probably the opinion of many in the present day, but it is none the less true that it does typically embody the emotional religious sentiment of the English middle classes of the fifties and sixties, in so far as that was genuine. This was shown by the enormous vogue it had. It was to be heard in every church, chapel, and parlour where there was a piano, at this time. It is one of those remarkable musical inspirations which seem to carry in them the whole atmosphere of a period. In its own way, a very different way certainly, it is in this respect comparable with *Ein' feste Burg* and the *Marseillaise*. The latter embody the virility of the German Reformation and the French Revolution respectively. *O Rest in the Lord* embodies the artificial, even where genuine, *bourgeois* emotional sweetness of the "place of worship" and the family parlour with its antimacassars and tea-urns of the English mid-nineteenth century.

Before taking leave of this world of the sixties – this world of tallow candles, snuffers, tea-urns, women's hair-nets and crinolines, men's broadcloth, stocks and pot-hats, four-post bedsteads, feather beds, hymns and oratorios – there is one question, which has always interested me, to be mooted. In how far are we to regard the religiosity, the theological and ecclesiastical interests, of the early and mid-Victorian period as the product of hypocrisy, and in how far was it genuine? That some of all this was genuine and a good deal of it deliberate hypocrisy I have no doubt whatever, but I should attribute the bulk of it to something between these two extremes which I should term *unconscious hypocrisy*. By unconscious hypocrisy I understand an attitude of mind which succeeds in persuading itself that it believes or approves certain things as it professes to do, while really *in foro conscientiae* this profession is dictated by a sense of its own interests, real or supposed. For instance, in discussing Free thought in religion or Radicalism in politics, as a makeweight to the conventional arguments against such

15

subversive doctrines, one often heard it thrown in, that if Freethought prevailed, or the political constitution were overthrown, there would be no security for property and its interests. Apart from the truth of theological doctrine or political theory, religion and the existing English constitution were necessary to keep the lower classes in order. Now it was this sort of remark, thrown in as above said as a makeweight, that first opened my eyes to the subconscious insincerity or unconscious hypocrisy of much of middle-class public opinion on these subjects. I could not escape the conviction that this secondary consideration, ostensibly a mere "aside" in the argument, was really the determining one in the formation of that opinion, albeit this fact was in many cases not consciously realized by the persons in question themselves.

A fairly typical illustration of what is said is afforded by the case of Dr. Colenso, Bishop of Natal, who in 1862 published a book on biblical criticism, the views contained in which are in their substance commonplaces to-day, but were at that time regarded as staggeringly subversive. The view that if the world in general came to disbelieve in the Mosaic authorship and the historicity of the Pentateuch, the world itself – *bien entendu* the mid-Victorian world of that date – would fall to pieces, was the current middle-class opinion. It seems scarcely credible to-day, but so it was. Hence the zeal with which the current theology with its dogma of biblical infallibility was defended at all costs. But in the case of the aforesaid Bishop of Natal there was an additional reason for using the cry of heresy as a means for effecting his discomfiture. Dr. Colenso was an eminently humane and just man, and in consequence was zealous in defending the rights of the native population of Natal against attempts of the British settlers to ride roughshod over those rights and to exploit the natives in their own interests. Hence the worthy Bishop was by no means a *persona grata* with the influential colonial magnates, or with the colonists generally, of his diocese. The charge of heresy was therefore a godsend to these gentry as a

16

weapon for getting him removed. Somehow or other they failed, owing, it was said, to their having played their cards badly with the Ecclesiastical Court which judged the case.

But notwithstanding the power of the middle-class ostracism of heterodox opinions, the decade of the sixties from its beginning onward showed an increasing number of books published, venturing to traverse the current conventional opinion of the day. My own childhood was padded towards the fag-end of the period of moral and intellectual slavery in question, in which the Calvinistic dogmas of Evangelicalism in religion and the Cobden-Bright dogmas of the Manchester School in economics and politics, modified by a snobbish reverence for authority in general and the upper classes, dominated the mentality of the whole social atmosphere. Those who want to know what it had been at an earlier period of the century, say during the forties and fifties, may consult the two volumes of the late Mr. A.W. Benn's excellent **History of English Rationalism in the Nineteenth Century**, or the short survey in Professor Bury's **History of Freedom of Thought** (pp.176-251). But though my youthful days were passed towards the end of the period in question, I experienced quite enough for it to have left an enduringly unpleasant reminiscence behind it. This is the more to be regretted as it affects one's memories of persons long since dead, whom one cannot altogether dissociate in one's mind from the at once morally repulsive and intellectually foolish beliefs they held, or professed to hold, and expected other people to hold. In themselves doubtless excellent, good-hearted people, their characters were poisoned and warped by the foulness and follies of their creed.

In the year 1864 we left Brighton and went to Hampstead. Here we led a life almost as retired as that of Brighton. I went to school for a short time, but my education was mainly conducted by private tuition. Here I began to take a definite interest in things, among others natural history, and especially entomology. Here also I made various acquaintances and two friendships, the

17

one a schoolboy friendship originating in common interests, butterfly collecting, etc. This was with the late Vivian Byam Lewes, who subsequently became the great chemist, whose lectures on the subject of practical chemistry in relation to the war are well known, and whose labours and studies in this department were only terminated by his sudden death at the comparatively early age of sixty-three in October 1915. Though close associates in boyhood and early youth, we subsequently drifted asunder owing to various causes, distance of residence, diversity of interests and other things, and I seldom saw Lewes after he had attained to manhood. While not possessed of any special intellectual qualities, Lewes was the type of the conscientious and thorough, if narrow, scientific specialist. He was the nephew of George Henry Lewes, the son of a brother of his who was killed as an officer of the Army Medical Corps in the Crimean War. His mother, a bright, intelligent woman, was a connexion of the Wellesley family. She much impressed me during my later boyhood owing to the freedom of her views on theological and political subjects. As regards the latter, it is true she clung to many of the prejudices of her time and class, with a tincture of aristocratic antipathies thrown in. This was still more the case with economic questions, where she was Manchester School to the backbone. Yet, strange to say, in spite of this strain of Whiggery and Manchesterism in her, this woman was one of the half-dozen persons of my acquaintance from whom a few years later I got some sympathy on the subject of the Commune. The barefaced misrepresentations and obviously unjust judgments of the *bourgeois* Press, and the brutalities of the *Versaillaise* soldiery, combined to disgust her with the enemies of the Commune. She also was prepared to recognize the high ideal underlying the movement and animating many of its advocates. Mrs. Edward Lewes was the first woman I had met having any pretensions to high culture or intelligence, and her intellectual superiority to other women I knew was a revelation to me.

The other friendship I made in Hampstead during the late

sixties was more enduring than that of Lewes, and happily subsists to this day. William Boulting, the distinguished authority on mediaeval and renaissance Italy, was, when I first met him, a student of medicine at University College. He used to attend with his father and mother a Baptist conventicle in Heath Street, Hampstead, in which my family also held what were known as "sittings." I used to have long walks with Boulting at this time, and one thing I can remember very well is that it was our delight on "sacrament" Sundays, while our elders were sacramentalizing within the walls of the chapel, to go for a walk on Hampstead Heath, and in that breezy atmosphere to indulge in free discussion of matters speculative, social and political. During a period of half a century I have never lost sight of Boulting for any long period, and our friendship has always remained unclouded. For long a medical practitioner in Hampstead, Boulting always found time for progressive self-culture, but it is only some twelve years ago that he was able to retire from practice and devote himself to the work of his life, the only work really congenial to him, viz. to his studies in Italian History, and to original thought in philosophy. A scrupulously exact and conscientious historical investigator, and an acute and careful philosophical thinker, I have always found the greatest intellectual stimulus and advantage from intercourse with him. May he live long to continue the good work he has done in his own special department of history, and to produce the work he is capable of in philosophy! Before leaving the subject I may mention, as illustrating the conscientious thoroughness of Boulting's historical work, that the Italian history published in one thick volume by Messrs. Routledge and Sons as an edition of Sismondi's "Italian Republics" is really a work of independent research. The editor, having found so much needing correction and alteration in its proportions to bring the original work of Sismondl up to date, decided to treat it in the manner of Wallenstein's war-steed, of which we are told "the head, neck, legs, and greater part of the body have been renewed; all the rest is the real horse." There is one thing I always admire and envy in

Boulting's work, and that is the faculty it shows for exact and careful research.

I have spoken above, in dealing with the early period of my childhood, of how, in spite of the mid-Victorian common sense, as embodied in my elders, I was imbued with the naive primitive belief of early man in the supernatural, as it is termed. About the age of eight or nine, it only required a very little suggestion to make me go to bed in abject fear of the appearance of a ghost, the devil, or some other unpleasant supernatural figure, out of the darkness by the bedside. Once I remember rousing the household by my screams, on being woke up by the squalling of cats immediately outside the window, believing the room to be full of hobgoblins. This state of mind was also stimulated by nightmares. I can well recall the peculiar horror of one of these, in which I saw seven gibbets on which were hanging seven beings howling. These seven beings were either seven great gaunt cats or seven thin, wizened, hideous old women – which, I could not tell. This dread of the dark and supernatural was, I suppose, common to the children of two or three generations ago, and was not infrequent with those of the time I am speaking of. With the modern child I imagine it hardly exists any more. A noteworthy point in connexion with it is, that this sense of the supernatural, which was the groundwork of the fear, in some cases survived sporadically and on rare occasions into earlier adult life. This has been confirmed by two or three friends of my generation. If I remember rightly, Goethe also has somewhere alluded to this feeling and its gradual cessation with advancing years, in his own life. The last instance of it in my case was soon after I was married to my first wife, when I was in the early twenties. We were looking for a house, and had seen one which seemed not unsuitable at West Croydon. There was nothing particular about the house, which was a comparatively small double-fronted one, with a good-sized walled garden, and dating probably from about the end of the first quarter of the nineteenth century. The taking of the house was noted as worthy of consideration, and it being somewhat late in the afternoon, we went home. But that same evening in the bedroom, the matter coming up again for discussion, my wife made the remark, "I don't know why it is, but somehow or other I feel there is something uncanny about the house. I can't help fancying that at this moment" – it being then about ten o'clock – "goblins might be holding their revels in that front room." "Very odd," I remarked; "I had a precisely similar feeling myself this afternoon on leaving that house!" I give this as it was a singular coincidence – a house not specially noteworthy in itself having excited similar fancies in two different persons at the same time. This was the last occasion on which I can remember having experienced a survival of the old childish feeling of the presence of the supernatural. In later life, as Goethe also has remarked, if I am not mistaken, in the passage above referred to in the **Wahrheit and Dichtung**, it is difficult even to recall what this old childish feeling was like.

With regard to the new quasi-scientific form assumed by the idea of the supernatural, supernormal, or occult (as one may choose to call it), as embodied in the labours and investigations of the "Society for Psychical Research," I am not entitled to offer a decided opinion, since I have not gone into the matter with any serious purpose. The reason for this is that I have always doubted, with regard to some of the chief subjects occupying the attention of this body, whether the probabilities of the case are sufficient to make it worth while to spend time and energy in investigating the subject. This of course, I know, is the commonplace opinion probably of the majority of educated mankind, but I hardly think the published results of the Society's work are sufficient, up to date, decisively to rebut it. In addition to this, there is a positive side to the matter, apart from the negative one of waste of time and energy, and that is the apparent tendency of such researches to deteriorate and debilitate the intellect. How often do we find men of fair average intelligence and strength of understanding who, beginning these "occult" studies in a perfectly reasonable and scientific spirit, after a time degenerate into credulous cranks. At the same time, as regards the Psychical Research Society, I would not deny that in certain departments of their investigations they have achieved some results. Notably is this the case in the matter of thought-transference. Here, they seem to have succeeded in establishing by their evidence, to say the least, a certain justification for the assumption of the possible interaction of individual minds directly and apart from the ordinary sense-channels. As concerns other departments of their studies touching the supernormal in its more strict sense, my own attitude, and it is shared, I think, by a good many persons of intelligence in the present day, might be described as an "agnostic" one, with a bias in favour of the negative opinion.

The dogmatism, in these matters, of the early and mid-Victorian man of education is now generally admitted to be scientifically indefensible, however much we may regard the balance of probabilities as being against the affirmative side. Speaking personally, my rationalistic conscience (using the word "rationalistic" in its traditional sense) sustains a far greater strain from the ordinary events of so-called "chance" in the world, by which, in defiance of all probabilities, as we generally understand them, one man is perennially lucky in the affairs of life, while the other (who probably belongs to a larger class) is perennially unlucky. It would seem as though what we call "chance," in events where human interests are involved, has as its peculiar characteristic the bring a respecter of persons, rather than, as in theory it ought, allowing its rain to descend equally "on the just and the unjust." In other words, events of this kind might seem to give the occultist a colourable pretence for his belief in the interference of supernormal or infra-normal (as one likes to regard it) intelligences or wills in the course of human affairs.[1] These commonplace and everyday events of luck and ill-luck pursuing particular individuals respectively, certainly seem to me, as far as they go, to tend more to weaken the rationalistic way of looking at things than the alleged "phenomena" (exceptional in any case) which interest Spiritists and Psychical Researchers. The special interest in these studies has its origin, of course, in the desire to arrive at an affirmative solution, on rational grounds, of the problem of the survival of personal identity and consciousness after death. I may mention here, in passing, the remark of a friend of mine who has dabbled considerably in Psychical Research, but who, unlike many others, has kept his mental balance, that none of the accredited evidence he had had before him afforded, in his opinion, any valid grounds for the assumption of the action of intelligences other than those "incarnated" ones concerned in the different experiments.

When about the age of fifteen my interest in music acquired a strong ascendancy over me. I began to study seriously musical theory with a view to devoting myself to composition. Although I broke off from time to time, I more than once resumed my endeavours in this direction, until subsequently I came to the conclusion that my inspiration fell so much below my aspiration in the domain of musical creativeness as to discourage me from pursuing the matter further. It was, however, some years later that I definitively resolved to abandon devoting myself to music as a career. Meanwhile, during the years (1875-6) that I was in Stuttgart, I zealously attended the Conservatorium for which that town is famous.

It was in 1870, just at the time of the outbreak of the Franco-German War, that we left Hampstead for Streatham, now a suburb of Greater London, but at that time still retaining some few surviving traces of its old rurality and village character. Thrale House, of Johnsonian memory, was then still standing. The Franco-German War of this year was the first public event that I followed with anything like continuous interest. The general sentiment in England with regard to the struggle was strongly pro-German. Nothing was known at that time of the "faked" telegram and of the true inwardness of the policy of Prussia and of Bismarck. The general notion was that the sole explanation of the war found expression in the fact that it was a gambler's last stake on the part of Napoleon III to rehabilitate himself by a great victory with the army, after the results of the plebiscite, recently held, had given such strong evidence of his waning popularity in French military circles.

The war, however, though it strongly interested me, was only the exordium to the drama of the Paris Commune of the following Spring, which proved a prominent landmark in my mental career. But of this more anon. During this winter of 1870-71 I did a considerable amount of reading in well-known books of the time, among which I may mention Lewes's **History of Philosophy** and **Life of Goethe**, Lecky's **Rationalism** and **European Morals**, Bain's psychological works, Spencer's **First Principles** and Mill's **Logic**.

The beginning of February 1871 saw the end of the war and the bases of an unsatisfactory future peace laid. But the internal condition of France, and especially Paris, continued disturbed. Finally, on the 18th of March the insurrection broke out in Paris which led to the establishment of the Commune, the first organized Government founded in the interests of the working class and having for its conscious aim the transformation of existing civilization in the direction of Socialism. I say in the direction of Socialism, for, though all those who took part in the Commune were almost entirely Socialists by instinct, yet they were not by any means all Socialists by understanding, in the scientific sense of to-day. Their general aspirations were towards a society of economical and political equality, but beyond this there was great nebulosity of view. The followers of Proudhon were still very numerous among the educated French working class and their representative men. But all this did not alter the fact that the Commune was, in essence, the outcome and embodiment of the first great movement of the working classes towards Socialism (for the abortive insurrection of June 1848 was too short-lived to count as such). Although at the time my own ideas of the aims of true social progress were nebulous enough, merely embracing political liberty and democracy together with

24

economic equality in a vague and abstract way, yet I could see the significance of the new movement in Paris from the first. My interest grew as events developed and culminated with the horrors of the *semaine sanglante*. I can well recall the tears I shed during these days, in secret and in my own room, over this martyrdom of all that was noblest (as I conceived it) in the life of the time. Henceforward I became convinced that the highest and indeed only true religion for human beings was that which had for its object the devotion to the future social life of humanity. The martyrs of the Commune who died, as one of there expressed it, *pour la solidarité humaine,* appealed to me a far nobler than any martyrs the Christian creed has had to show. the Communist believed that his end at the hands of the *Versaillaise* soldiery meant the extinction of his personality, but perhaps a step towards the realization of his ideal, and in this belief he faced death. The Christian martyr, on the other hand, we may presume, was sincerely convinced according to the tenets of his creed that his death at the hands of the executioner opened for his personality the gates of a paradise of never-ending bliss.

These considerations, only intensified by the foul abuse and lies with which the *bourgeois* Press assailed the Commune and all those connected with it, made an ineffaceable impression upon me. The idea of human progress as the proper object of religion led me some time after this to attach myself somewhat, although I never formally joined it, to the Positivist body, the leaders of which at that time were Dr. Richard Congreve, Mr. Frederic Harrison, Professor Beesly, and Dr. Bridges. Professor Beesly having died in old age recently, Mr. Frederic Harrison is the only living survivor of this group. I was the more attracted to the Positivists from the fact that they were the only organized body of persons at that time in the country who had the courage systematically to defend the movement of which the Commune was the outcome, as well as the actions of the Commune and its adherents themselves. Exception must be made, of course, of the small circle that gathered round Karl Marx and formed the nucleus of the British Branch of the International Association. But the old International, notwithstanding its influence on the Continent, had never any real hold on the English intellectual or working classes, and it is extremely doubtful whether more than a few, more or less in the inner circle, fully realized what the Commune meant, or sympathized with its aims. For the rest, the other popular movements of the day, which centred round Charles Bradlaugh and the National Secular Society, were steeped in Manchester School economic prejudices and were thoroughly insular in their general outlook. As a consequence of this they were mostly unsympathetic to the French "Red Republican" party, as it was then the fashion to call it. The Positivists, on the contrary, manfully espoused the cause of the Commune in the **Fortnightly Review**, at that time edited by Mr. John (now Lord) Morley. The same may be said of the weekly journal, **The Examiner**, originally established by Albany Fonblanque, and to which in its early days John Stuart Mill was a regular contributor. It was edited, at the time of which I speak, by my elder contemporary and friend, the late Mr. Fox Bourne.

The latter, although a thorough Manchester School man and political Radical of the Cobden-Bright type, was also thoroughly honest up to his lights, and respected the honesty and self-sacrifice of those who had suffered for their ideal in Paris, little as he might appreciate that ideal itself. He has informed me that during the period of the Commune and for some time after he was a frequent caller at Marx's house in Maitland Park, Haverstock Hill, where he received the true account of things which were taking place, and after the Commune had been suppressed he met many of the refugees who used to visit there. It thus came about, as stated, that **The Examiner** bravely defended the honesty and courageous enthusiasm of the Commune and its adherents.

As is well known, the following year, 1872, saw what was practically the wind-up of the old International (founded in 1864) at the Hague Congress. Its end was the work of Marx and his friend Engels. The latter stated, in a speech closing the International Socialist Congress held at Zurich in 1893 that they felt the situation to be becoming on the Continent too dangerous for the old organization to be maintained. They feared, he said, lest its maintenance might mean the wrecking of the liberty and perhaps the lives of too many valuable workers for the cause under the existing conditions in many European countries.

I have dwelt upon this matter of the Commune at some length, as it had a strong influence upon the whole course of my thought on things social and political, and led ultimately to my becoming a convinced Socialist. At the time being, of course, it was the heroism of the Communards in their championing of the cause of the people, of the economically oppressed and downtrodden, that fired my youthful imagination.

During the early years of the seventies I continued my studies in various directions, until in August 1875 I went to Stuttgart, where, still with a view of devoting myself to music, especially composition, I joined the Conservatorium. Stuttgart was at that tune still a quaint old town as regards its central portion, although a circle of new streets and buildings was already sufficiently in evidence on its outer fringe. I remained in Stuttgart for :somewhat over a year, mixing freely with all sorts and conditions of men. From Stuttgart I went down South into French Switzerland, residing for two or three months in the house of a *pasteur* at the little village of La Sarraz, in the Canton de Vaud, not very far from Lausanne. I returned home to Streatham in the Autumn of the year 1876. A year later I married. My wife was the collateral descendant of John Hoole, the contemporary and friend of Dr. Johnson, and the well-known translator of Tasso and other poets of the Italian Renaissance.

With the few details given above I may appropriately close the present chapter of reminiscences belonging to the period of childhood and youth. What is known as the mid-Victorian period was soon to lapse into the late-Victorian period.

# Notes

1. For instance, as illustrating the apparent impish *design* in chance, there is the well-known phenomenon of the successful lottery ticket – the almost invariable coincidence that if the ticket be lost, destroyed, or otherwise become unavailable, it unfailingly wins the first prize.

# II. Men and the Movements of the Early Eighties

In the Summer of 1880 I received a call to Berlin to act as assistant correspondent to the late Dr. Carl Abel, who was at that time engaged as chief correspondent of the **Standard**. I well remember how the room in Dr. Abel's residence which served as office overlooked the study of the late Professor Droysen, and how from my desk the Professor was to be seen inditing his historical works. Bamberger, the celebrated National-Liberal member of the Reichstag, lived in a house standing in its own garden, also nearly in front of us, while the well-known friend of Heine, Fanny Lewald, resided not far off. In the November of this year 1880 I went to report the festivities connected with the restoration of Cologne Cathedral. Although the completion of the twin spire was undoubtedly carried out as ably as possible in accordance with the original plan, I, for my part, quite share William Morris's regrets for the unfinished condition, with the quaint "mediaeval crane" still remaining where it was left by the members of the old guild of masons in the sixteenth century.

Old Gallenga, the well-known writer on the staff of **The Times**, was also in Cologne reporting the proceedings. An amusing incident occurred in connexion with Gallenga. I was sitting next to him one day at luncheon in our hotel, and on the other side was a pompous Prussian. As, after the meal, we were rising from the table, our pompous Prussian addressed Gallenga, asking whether he were not the correspondent of **The Times**. Gallenga, somewhat taken aback, admitted that he was. "Then, sir, are you aware that you have grossly insulted the whole German nation?" Gallenga replied that he was not conscious of having committed any indiscretion of the kind. "Do you not know then, sir," retorted the pompous Prussian, "that you described the assembly at the celebration as wearing shabby overcoats?" As Gallenga told me afterwards, all that he had said was that the brilliant uniforms of the military made a striking contrast with the overcoats of the civilians, and that the contrast gave the latter almost a shabby appearance.

An interesting personality I met in Berlin at that time was the late Edward von Hartmann, the author of a book which had an enormous run in its day and was translated into all the important European languages, **Die Philosophie des Unbewussten (The Philosophy of the Unconscious)**, Hartmann was lame and could not get out much. I was frequently at his house and had many a discussion on philosophical questions with him. Especially I remember talking over the possibility of a corporate social consciousness being in the womb of time and evolution. This idea was new to him, and he seemed rather at a loss as to his attitude towards it. He was a good amateur vocalist and used to sing the baritone parts in Wagner, especially *Wie oft in Meeres tiefstem Schlund* from the *Fliegender Holländer.* My friendship with Von Hartmann at this time has always been a pleasant memory with me, and I only regret that after leaving Berlin I never saw him again. He died early in 1914.

On Dr. Abel's retirement in 1881 from the correspondentship of the **Standard**, I left Berlin and returned to England, where I fixed myself for the next few years, at Croydon. This period, that of the first half of the eighty decade, was an important turning-point in the intellectual and social life of England. It was in the Spring of 188t that Hyndman founded the "Democratic Federation," which subsequently became the "Social Democratic Federation" and – in later years "The British Socialist Party." The Bradlaugh struggle with the House of Commons was a prominent feature of these years. Charles Bradlaugh was still the *bête noire* of the British propertied classes, who had the idea that he was a desperate revolutionist, whose subversive teaching was calculated to place the institution of private property in jeopardy. This notion was not broken down until his great debate with Hyndman at St. James's Hall on April 20, 1881, in which he appeared as the champion of the existing order of society and the bitter opponent of Socialism and of all reforms tending in the direction of Socialism. But it is singular to note that the change in public opinion as regards Bradlaugh was also symptomatic of a change in the attitude of British sentiment towards theological heterodoxy and disbelief in general. Bradlaugh, who was President of the "National Secular Society" and a militant Atheist lecturer, had for this reason alone hitherto been their special bogy, Now, on his coming down firmly on the side of the sanctity of the existing economic social order and of private property in the means of production, they willingly forgave, or at least condoned, his Atheism. But this matter of Bradlaugh was really, as already said, no more than a symptom of a change in the whole attitude of the British mind towards religion. The change had begun in the later sixties, and was marked by the growing popularity of the works of Darwin, Spencer, Lecky, and others, but it was only beginning, and, as pointed out in the last chapter, Evangelical dogma, church- and chapel-going, and all that that implies, continued to rule the roost with the vast majority of the middle-class population of these islands. During the seventies undoubtedly a further advance was made towards the breakdown of this obscurantism, but it was not till the early eighties that it can be said to have definitively and finally collapsed. To those of the younger generation it is to-day inconceivable what the social ostracism, backbiting, and persecution of unpopular opinion meant in the sixties, and even, though to a lesser degree, in the seventies, of the last century. Well, as we have said, this state of things seemed to break down fairly completely with more or less suddenness between the years 1880 and 1885. The taking of Charles Bradlaugh, in a manner, into the bosom of British Respectability about the close of this period was only one of the straws slowing the shift in the direction of the social current. Bradlaugh, it was true, had pronounced against Socialism, but he had not gone to the Canossa of "Respectability" in the matter of Atheism. In this respect British Respectability met him more than half way. For the rest, the capitalist classes of this country, had they had any sense, might have known years before that Bradlaugh's views on social and economic questions were not dangerous to them, from his attitude towards the "International Association" and the Paris Commune. It is a fact worth noting before leaving the subject that the *effective* movement for freedom of thought and toleration of opinion in this country began almost exclusively from the literary and cultured side. Freethought among the masses, as represented by the National Secular Society, continued till the period in question to be regarded not merely as crude and coarse in its inception and expression, as indeed it very often was, but as socially disreputable. It was not till the early eighties and the prosecution of Foote for blasphemy that the better-educated middle classes began to have sense and justice enough to see the movement from below for freedom of thought, commonly known as Secularism, for what it was, namely, the plucky effort of men of the small middle and working classes to emancipate themselves, up to their lights, from the thraldom of an encumbering and galling superstition, fatal to all advance in knowledge and to all independent intellectual effort. Since the early eighties, social persecution in matters of opinion, whether theological or otherwise, has happily ceased to be a stumbling-block in the path of the intellectual and general progress of this country.

In 1882 I joined the Democratic Federation, rather more than a year after its foundation. But before entering upon the history of Socialism in England, the beginnings of which were identified with the organization in question, I may perhaps say a few words about some men whose acquaintance I made some little while before this. Hermann Jung was a working watchmaker by trade, and a French Swiss (Vaudois) by origin. He used to live and carry on his business in Charles Street, Clerkenwell, where I on several occasions had conversations with him. Jung was an extraordinary autodidact. He had lived in London for many years-indeed, since he was quite a young man. Speaking English, French, and German alike fluently, before long he came into close touch with political refugees of the '48 movement, and made the acquaintance of Marx and his circle. He soon got to be one of Marx's intimate disciples, and when the International Association was founded, in the Autumn of 1864, he took his place among the most enthusiastic spirits of the London section. He used to have much to tell of his relations with Marx, for whom he had the profoundest admiration. They finally quarrelled over the break-up of the old International. The reason of the difference was Jung's disapproval of the arbitrary and, as he considered, unfair methods adopted by Marx and his friend Engels at the Hague Congress of 1872 to get rid of the disciples of Bakunin and other non-Marxian and anti-Marxian elements in the body. The Marxists, as is well known, succeeded in overriding all opposition and getting their motions carried, the most important of these being the transference of the General Council of the Association to New York. This meant, of course, as it was intended to mean, the death-blow of the old organization. The reasons given for the Marxists' action by Friedrich Engels, who was probably its chief promoter, at the Zurich Congress of 1893, have been stated on a former page. The immediate result of the steps taken at the initiation of Marx and his friends was the split up of the International into three or four fragments, each claiming to represent the original body. Hermann Jung, although theoretically as strict a Marxist as ever, sympathized strongly with the opposition parties and with their determination to treat the resolutions of the Hague Congress, obtained by intrigue and unfair means, as he viewed the matter, as null and void. The fragments dragged on a precarious existence for a few years, but by the end of the decade of the seventies the old International had definitively ceased to exist.

I first made the acquaintance of Hermann Jung at one of the meetings of the London Dialectical Society, then held in Langham Hall, Great Portland Street. The lecturer was the late Mr. Leonard Montefiore, his subject being *German Social Democracy*. He treated the matter from the then conventional

33

middle-class point of view as a somewhat foolish aberration of the masses, although he strongly denounced the anti-Socialist coercion laws, the enactment of which Bismarck had just succeeded in procuring. The treatment of the subject in the somewhat *de haut en bas* manner of the lecturer brought Jung, as soon as the lecture was concluded, to his feet in a fury. The result was one of the most effective and rousing speeches in defence of Socialism I have ever heard. There was no mistake about it. Hermann Jung was a born orator. When I knew him he seldom took part in public meetings, but in his younger days, when he was an active propagandist, he must have been extraordinarily effective and powerful.

Poor Hermann Jung came to a sad end. Among the numerous persons who, claiming to be political refugees, always found a welcome in his workshop, was a French criminal who, while Jung was bending over his bench, struck him a blow on the head with some sharp instrument which killed him at once. The object was robbery, but his assailant, although he fled from the house, did not succeed in escaping, being caught red-handed, and in due course tried and executed.

Another man with whom I became acquainted through Jung was the then Socialist and subsequent Anarchist, Johannes Most. At the time I first met him, at the end of the seventies, he had quarrelled with the leaders of the Social Democratic party in Germany, and was editing a paper of his own, **Die Freiheit**, in a street off Tottenham Court Road. Most was rather an insignificant-looking man, but with a fund of unmistakble energy in him. His Socialism had been much influenced by the writings of Eugen Dühring, Professor of Political Economy in the Berlin University, a man now almost forgotten, but who at that time aspired to play a role as a theorist of Socialism in competition with Marx, and who had a considerable vogue for a few years among a section of the German Social Democrats, especially in Berlin. His fame now rests upon the polemical treatise of Friedrich Engels directed against him, in which his pretensions were effectually and finally disposed of.

Most became notorious in England through his prosecution, after the slaying of the Czar Alexander 11 by the 1Nihilists in March 1881. In his article in the **Freiheit**, Most not only justified the "removal" of Alexander II in particular, or Czars in general, but advocated a similar treatment for the heads of all States "from St. Petersburg to Washington" inclusive. The Liberal English Government of the time, with the late Sir William Harcourt as Home Secretary, probably influenced from Berlin by the German authorities, of whom Bismarck was then the head, undertook a prosecution. Most, as is well known, was sentenced to eighteen months' imprisonment with hard labour. His treatment in prison seems to have been vindictive and scandalous. This took place immediately after my return from Berlin in the Spring of 1881, and the last time I ever saw Most was in the clock at Bow Street during the police court proceedings before the trial at the Old Bailey. He subsequently went to America, where he became more than ever Anarchist and Terrorist in his views, and published a paper in this sense which again brought him into trouble, this time with the American governing powers. In 1907 he died in New York.

Another well-known though very different figure to whom I was introduced by Hermann Jung; was Prince Kropotkin, whose picturesque and benevolent-looking head has since become familiar in many English social circles. At that time he had only just come over to England, and, indeed, had not very long escaped from Russia. He arrived, however, immediately from Geneva, where he had for some time been editing his paper, **Le Revolté**. His theoretical Anarchism furnished a fertile subject of controversy between us on more than one occasion. I well remember a long walk I had with him one day in the early summer of 1882 from Croydon to Leatherhead, during which he expounded his views on the Social Revolution and had much to say against Marx and other leaders of the main Social Democratic movement. Prince Kropotkin subsequently obtained distinction in

35

this country for the exceptionally able popular articles on the results of up-to-date science which he wrote in the **Nineteenth Century** and elsewhere. He still, I believe, retains in its essentials his old standpoint in social and political matters, which he has endeavoured to illustrate in more than one book published since then. His industry and accuracy in collecting facts are undeniable, and especially in his work **Mutual Aid** there are some just and useful aperçus, but I fail to see that they point in the direction of the theory of Social Anarchism I understand him still to hold. Kropotkin always struck me, when I conversed with him, as having a lingering belief in the individualist-introspective ethics of the ordinary *bourgeois* Puritanism – with the idea of individual self-immolation through asceticism, in its various modes, as having an intrinsic value in itself. As regards Economics, he insisted on the theory that concentration in industrial processes was only a passing phase in industrial evolution, which had reached its greatest intensity during the period in which steam was the main motive-power in production, but that the full development of the era of electricity would show a return, in a large measure, to the old small industry of individual production, owing to the fact that, unlike steam-power, electricity can be split up without losing its efficiency. It is now more than thirty-five years ago since Prince Kropotkin expounded this, to me, novel doctrine, in the course of our peregrinations among the Surrey hills. The subsequent history of Industrial Progress has certainly falsified the prognostications suggested by the theory. The answer to it, indeed, is obvious, even assuming the scientific basis of Kropotkin's view to have been adequate, or indeed sustainable at all in the present day, as to which I am not competent to judge. The concentration of manufacturing processes, with the division of labour involved therein, began long before the steam era – before, indeed, any motricity other than that more or less immediately produced and controlled by the hand of the workman was so much as thought of. Yet, notwithstanding this, the concentration of production under one roof and one direction progressively and steadily made headway from the second half of the sixteenth century onward in ever more branches of industry, little by little supplanting the old individual craftsmanship. The introduction of complex machinery on a large scale, and still more of steam-motricity at the end of the eighteenth and beginning of the nineteenth centuries, certainly accelerated the complete domination of the centralizing process in all branches of production, thereby inaugurating what we call the "Great Industry" of the industrial revolution. But steam-driven machinery most assuredly did not create the tendency by which the principle of concentration, with its correlative division of labour, has progressively superseded the individual handicraft industry from the close of the Middle Ages onward. Hence, I say, even assuming the accuracy of Kropotkin's forecast as to the possibilities inherent in the application of electricity to industrial processes, by which in certain departments of production (for it could, of course, only apply to certain departments) a return to the methods of the small industry might take place, yet the same cause-the greater effectiveness of combined and organized over isolated labour-which originally gave rise to the supplanting of handicraft methods by concentration of production under one roof, with division of its processes, must continue to operate in realizing the same tendency, just as it did before the introduction of steam and modern machinery.

About this time I began seriously to study Marx's great work **Das Kapital**, and towards the end of 1881 I wrote a short monograph on the subject of Marx and his work in a monthly review called **Modern Thought**, now long since defunct. This notice, although by no means faultless as regards its accuracy, pleased Marx and Engels. Marx himself, being at the time too ill to write, sent me his thanks and many appreciative messages in a letter written by his daughter Eleanor. The great founder of the theoretic basis of modern scientific socialist economy lived for more than a year after this incident, but he was away for his health during a considerable portion of the time, and I never met him. The circumstance of the article referred to, however, led to an invitation a short time after Marx's death in March 1883 from Friedrich Engels to visit him, a visit which began an acquaintance and friendship lasting till his own death in 1895.

Friedrich Engels I consider to be one of the most remarkable men of his time – a man of encyclopaedic reading and of considerable up-to-date knowledge in all branches of science – anything that Engels had to say or to write always had its points and was worth consideration, even in subjects of which he was not complete master, as he was of Political Economy. But Engels had his limitations intellectually. For one thing he was somewhat hide-bound to the shibboleths of the old dogmatic materialism. He, like Marx, had sprung from the left wing of the old Hegelian school, of which Ludwig Feuerbach was the most popular literary exponent. This school, while retaining the Hegelian Logic or Dialectic, strenuously repudiated Metaphysics and all interest in the problem of Metaphysics. The reaction against the Idealism of the main current of German philosophy, as the latter existed to well-nigh the end of the earlier half of the nineteenth century, led, as might have been expected, to the assertion of a somewhat crude and dogmatic materialism. This was very noticeable in Marx and Engels. In their case, it received a special colouring from their economic and historical studies. Its best known result was the so-called "Materialist theory of history." This meant the reduction of all the changes in the development of human society to economic terms. It meant, that is, that all political, moral, aesthetic, religious, intellectual evolution is to be regarded as the reflex merely of economic change, by which is understood change in the mode of the production of wealth or of the distribution of wealth in other words, of the manner in which the material modes of existence of the community are determined.

According to the old theory, the dominant factor in the life of any age or people was always its speculative or religious beliefs. This theory may now be fairly regarded as exploded. It is to the everlasting credit of Marx and Engels to have pointed out

38

the importance of the material or economic basis of society in moulding and influencing that society's life and destinies. But what the Marxian school fails to recognize is that this one factor, important and even fundamental though it be, is not by itself necessarily the sole determining cause in social evolution. Moral, intellectual, and other non-material factors also play their part, and it may be quite as important a part, in determining the current of human affairs. In one age and under one set of circumstances, the economic factor may play the leading role; in another age and under another set of circumstances, a religious, moral, or political belief or conviction may occupy the leading place and economic conditions a comparatively secondary one. In one or two articles written quite at the end of his life and published after his death, Engels himself would seem to have to some extent recognized the inadequacy of what is regarded as the orthodox Marxist position. But Engels, as I knew him, held to the theory in all its one-sidedness. Speaking generally, Engels showed a tendency to regard all other studies and departments of knowledge, so to say, as appendices of his own special department, i.e. Political Economy. I have often noticed this when conversing with him. I suppose we must regard it as the necessary drawback of the specialist, this tendency to regard everything else as subordinate to his specialism. For instance, if you spoke with Engels on some purely philosophical or psychological problem, he could only envisage it as the expression of some social antagonism, or as the point of view of some special economic class, at some special moment of its development-it might be the decaying feudal class, or the rising capitalist class, or what not. He could not, it seemed, see that the problem had an intrinsic quality, meaning, and interest of its own and in itself. The whole historical course of speculative thought was to be interpreted economically as the varying expression of class aspiration or antagonism. I remember one day, when discussing with him the materialist doctrine of history, challenging him to deduce the appearance, in the Roman Empire of the second century, of the Gnostic sects, and the success of many of them for a time among the populations of the larger cities of the Mediterranean basin, from the economic conditions of the Roman world at the time. He admitted he could not do this, but suggested that by tracing the matter further back you might arrive at some economic explanation of what he granted was an interesting side-problem of history. What he meant by this retrospective interpretation I am unable to say, for the conversation was interrupted by the arrival of visitors and was not resumed.

Marx and Engels, as is well known, were always recognized as a sort of court of ultimate appeal by the Social Democratic party, in spite of the fact that on one occasion, that of the negotiations with the Lassalleans before the Erfurt Congress, their views were overridden by the actual leaders of the party in Germany, Bebel and Liebknecht. But this was quite exceptional, and I believe, indeed, the only case of such a thing occurring. As a general rule, Marx and Engels were final arbiters in questions of party policy. After Marx's death this role became naturally concentrated in the person of Engels. Though prepared to give due weight to the practical exigencies of the situation on all occasions, the old colleague and survivor of Marx till the last held to the view that the social revolution could not be inaugurated otherwise than by the methods of forcible insurrection – least of all in Germany. I have more than once heard him say that as soon as one man in three, i.e. one-third, of the German army actually in service could be relied on by the party leaders, revolutionary action ought to be taken. Engels would certainly not have recognized the Socialism (?) of Scheidemann, Südekum, Noske, and the rest of the present "Revisionist" crew constituting the actual majority of the party representation in the Reichstag as anything else than reaction in its worst form.

The earlier career of Engels was interesting in many ways. Born at Barmen, in Rhenish Prussia, in 1820, after completing his studies at the University of Berlin he was sent over to England to Manchester, to look after a cotton-spinning business in which his father, who was a man of some means, had a share. It was here that his interest in Social problems received its most powerful stimulus, from the conditions in the housing and life of the labouring class which he found prevailing there. His investigations resulted in the production of his first work, **Die Lage der arbeitenden Klassen in England (The Position of the Working Classes in England)**. From this residence in Manchester, dating from when he was quite a young man, Engels acquired a thorough acquaintance with English life, manners, and thought. He had some interesting experiences to relate concerning English society and ways during the first half of the nineteenth century – the time, as he was wont to express it, before salad oil appeared on English dinner-tables. He related to me how, smoking at that time being regarded as more or less "bad form" in society, he was on one occasion requested by the master of the house where he was dining, who, notwithstanding the shocked proprieties of his daughters, was addicted to his pipe after dinner, to join him for the purpose of a tranquil smoke in the kitchen! – and this was a well-to-do Manchester manufacturer who lived in a good house! Again, he had reminiscences of port and sherry as the only wine drunk by or known to the average Englishman. This fact was humorously illustrated by the contemporary translation into English of the opening line of Leporello's drinking song in *Don Giovanni* as "Come, let us be merry with port and with sherry" the idea of being merry with any other wine, save perhaps with the rare and costly exception of champagne, being inconceivable to the English mind of the period. He had a story also of how he, wearing a beard, at that time regarded as a great eccentricity, being worn by few Englishmen, when he went out for a stroll on Sunday morning would meet occasionally a fellow bearded man, who would greet him with something like a religious fervour, and perhaps anon another. These bearded eccentricities were the surviving followers of the notorious Johanna Southcott, who affirmed that she would be delivered of a supernatural being, Shiloh, on the 19th of October 1814, but who died of dropsy a few days after instead. Her followers, who were said to have originally numbered one hundred thousand, did not become extinct before the middle of the nineteenth century. They regarded the wearing of the beard as a sign of the elect. As illustrating the universality of church- and chapel-going on a Sunday in the England of the forties and fifties of the last century, Engels told of a conversation which took place at the house of one of his Manchester acquaintances during a midday dinner (they did not call it luncheon in those days in middle-class circles) to which he was invited one Sunday. The talk, as was then inevitable, turned on the morning's preachers, and Engels, on being asked what "place of worship" he attended, replied that he always took a walk in the country on Sunday morning, that being, he found, the best way of spending the early hours of his leisure day. On hearing this, his host addressed him with the remark, "You seem to hold peculiar religious views, Mr. Engels – somewhat Socinian, I think!" The observation is amusingly significant of the notions prevalent at that period, when "somewhat Socinian" was about the extreme limit of theological heterodoxy conceivable to the respectable middle-class mind. The notion of the devout Atheist Engels being "somewhat Socinian" is also very funny.

It is noteworthy that Friedrich Engels, notwithstanding his long residence in England and acquaintance with the English people, never in himself became completely anglicized. He always retained to the last his German individuality. It is singular too that Engels, with all his versatility and literary capacity, never produced any great independent literary work. His writings mainly consisted of articles, with occasional longer essays, the most important of which have been collected and published in German under the auspices of Bernstein, Kautzky, and Mehring. His independent publications during his lifetime were mostly of the nature of expanded brochures. Such was **The Position of the Working Classes in England**. His greatest literary achievement was undoubtedly his work against Dühring. But here again we have no more than an expanded polemical essay. This is much to be regretted. Had Engels undertaken to embody his wide knowledge and often extremely keen intellectual insight in a substantive and systematic form, he would undoubtedly have produced something of real and permanent value for the Socialist thought not merely of the present time but of the future. As it is, the form which his writings took suggests a danger of their more or less falling into oblivion within a generation or two from the time of his death.

Like other men of considerable intellectual capacity, Friedrich Engels had very markedly the proverbial "defects of his qualities." Together with his friend Marx, and like other Socialist leaders I could name, he was a thoroughly bad judge of men. Moreover, he was absurdly jealous of any one he did not know himself entering into any close personal relations of friendship with Marx. An apt illustration of this is afforded by the case of my friend H.M. Hyndman. Hyndman had become acquainted with Marx, and the acquaintanceship had ripened into a cordial friendship. It would appear (I take Engels' own version of the matter as the basis of my remarks) as though Engels had no sooner perceived that Hyndman had made an impression on Marx, than he sought to undermine the friendly relations between the two men. The pretext, for I am afraid we must regard it only as a pretext, was found in the fact that Hyndman early in 1882 had published a little book entitled **England for All**, in which he put, in a popular and very brief form, the main economic positions of modern Socialism, derived of course from Marx, but without mentioning their source by name. In this it should be understood Hyndman did not pretend to claim them for his own, but admitted that he was indebted for them to an eminent foreign Economist. His reason for not referring directly to Marx at that moment was, I understand, that the intimation of their having been made if not "in Germany," at least by a Jew of German birth, might prejudice their reception, new and unfamiliar as they were, in this country of insular prejudices. Be this as it may, the omission of Marx's name afforded the excuse for Engels to persuade Marx that Hyndman's friendship covered a designing intent to suck Marx's brains and obtain the credit in English-speaking countries for the results of Marx's work. Marx at first excused Hyndman to Engels on the ground that the book was written specially for certain London Radical clubs and he believed was not in general circulation. Thereupon Engels orders the brochure from his bookseller, and a few days after proceeds triumphantly to Maitland Park, holding it aloft and shaking it as he advances to meet Marx. Marx yielded to Engels' blandishments. Result, a "coolness" which practically ended the relations between Marx and Hyndman.

Another instance of Engels' womanish prejudice against a man to whom he had taken a dislike, based on preposterously inadequate grounds, is afforded by his attitude towards that excellent Socialist, Adolphe Smith. The origin of this antipathy, as stated by Engels himself, almost passes belief in its absurdity. Adolphe Smith, as is well known, took part in the Commune. On his arrival in London, after his escape from Paris early in June 1871, he started a series of lectures in defence of the Commune, and, as was only to be expected – considering the attitude of the Press and the ferocity of the hatred worked up among the British bourgeoisie against the Commune and all who defended it – these lectures, although exciting some interest at first, soon ceased to pay their way, and had to be discontinued, with a loss to Smith, a comparatively poor man, of time and money. Among the known sympathizers with the cause to whom an announcement of the lectures was sent were Marx and Engels, who duly attended them on more than one occasion. Engels himself admitted Smith's defence of the Commune to have been satisfactory. But it so happened that shortly after the cessation of the lectures Smith was one of the signatories to a protest against the somewhat high-handed action of the Marxian party on the central committee of the International. This protest, in which there were certain, what we should call now Anarchistic elements, involved, contained expressions which Smith in his maturer years has allowed were crude and ill-conceived. He also admits his having signed the manifesto at all to have been dictated by youthful enthusiasm, genuine but not overwise. Now, Adolphe Smith's participation in the document in question was a thing Engels never forgave the unfortunate Smith. It rankled in his mind for a quarter of a century, until the day of his death. But this was not all. On the basis of his resentment Engels built up the following preposterous hypothesis, which he retailed as fact. Smith, as we have seen, had sent himself and Marx a syllabus of his lectures requesting their attendance and recommendation to friends. The lectures proved a financial failure. Smith, according to Engels, regarded their failure as being due to lack of interest shown by himself, Marx, and their friends in the enterprise. Thereupon, vowing vengeance in his wrath, the malignant Smith, as Engels declared, drew up and circulated the wicked manifesto attacking the Marxian policy! *Hinc illae lacrymae!* Such was the absurdly malevolent construction Engels chose to put upon two utterly disconnected facts. Any one who knows Adolphe Smith must recognize, of course, how entirely impossible is the assumption of Engels and how utterly inconsistent it is with the character of the man in question. Adolphe Smith, it should be observed, is one whose record for unostentatious and ungrudging work for the Socialist movement has been exceeded by few. Other men have got at least a certain amount of kudos and public recognition for their work. Adolphe Smith's work has been mostly of a kind unrecognized by the general public. So bitter was Engels' animosity, that on one occasion towards the end of his life, when Smith had been persuaded by some mutual friends to join them in a call on Engels, the latter could not restrain himself in his own house from the most ill-mannered conduct towards the man he so bitterly and unreasonably hated.

Another instance on the other side of Engels' utter incapacity to judge men was his vehement championship of Dr. Edward Aveling, the husband (in free marriage) of Eleanor, the daughter of his friend Marx. No amount of evidence of Aveling's

45

delinquencies in money matters, or of the untrustworthiness and complete unreliability of his character generally as a man, would induce Engels to cease placing his trust in him. What was worse, he was continually trying to foist him as a leader upon the English Socialist and Labour movement. His sincerity in this, as in the rest of his actions, is undoubted, but is one more illustration of the very serious defects of his qualities in this, in many respects, great man.

In giving the foregoing incidents tending to show the unpleasant sides of Friedrich Engels, I am not actuated by any mere love of scandal, but by the fact that the incidents narrated have not been without influence on the International Socialist movement. Engels' fierce dislike of Hyndman, for instance, did not end with his achievement of causing a breach between Hyndman and Marx, but continued to work its evil influence after Marx's death in exciting a distrust and prejudice against Hyndman among the best of the "old guard" of the German Social Democratic party, such as Liebknecht, Bebel, Singer, Kautzky, and others; and although the ill-feeling was got over in some cases, notably that of old Liebknecht, who subsequently became on very friendly terms with Hyndman, yet for a long time it distinctly caused a certain strain in the relations between the old German party of twenty or thirty years ago and the only English party really representing Marxian Socialism, i.e. the Social Democratic Federation.

Similarly with Adolphe Smith. Although, owing to the relative positions of the two men in English Socialism, its effect was not so obvious in his case, it nevertheless give rise to most unjust suspicions against one of the worthiest and most disinterested members of the English party. Yet again, Engels' exaltation of Aveling and his representing of him as a leading figure in the British Socialist party, which he never was, often gave occasion, in its turn, to an entirely false estimate on the Continent of the situation in the British movement. These things being so, I hold it well that the above unpleasant facts, although in themselves of a purely personal nature, should be placed on record for the benefit of the future historian, when he may come to deal with the international side of Socialism as it stood during the last two decades of the nineteenth century.

# III. On Century-End Literature, Art and Philosophy

THE expression *fin de siècle*, which sprang up originally, if I remember rightly, in the early eighties, became very popular as the century more nearly approached its close. It had, indeed, an actual significance. As already observed in a previous chapter, the early eighties did undoubtedly mark the culmination of a great change in English popular thought. Perhaps the year 1884 may be specially mentioned in this connexion. It was in this year that the modern English Socialist movement really began to take root and excite interest in the country. With this, however, I propose to deal at length in another chapter. But in other ways also the advent of the mind of a new generation showed itself about this time. The old English Puritanism ceased to concern itself primarily with theological dogma, but turned its principal attention to practical issues and questions of conduct. Its view of moral problems of course centred in the old bourgeois Puritan notions. The circumference of morality still mainly circled round the question of sex relations: sexual abstention under the name of "Social Purity" bulked largely, as it has always done with this type of mind, as the great moral achievement. The late W.T. Stead was its chief literary and journalistic coryphaeus, and the Rev. Hugh Price Hughes its prophet and priest in pulpit and on platform. The movement was also mixed up with Feminism, with which I intend also to deal in a later chapter.

Now was the time of the great Browning "boom." Browning clubs sprang up in all cultured middle-class circles. Robert Browning was proclaimed as the poet of the age, and the study of his poems was declared by many enthusiasts as a liberal education in itself. Altogether, in the years of these early eighties it became clear that the culture, using the word in its widest sense, of mid-Victorian England had lost its savour and survived its influence. The late-Victorian period which ushered in the

49

twentieth century was already in full swing. The contrast between the new culture, as we may term it, and that of the so-called early Victorian period of the forties and fifties, became very marked indeed. Dickens, to take an example from fictional literature, began to get distinctly old-fashioned as the society of his heyday died off. Even his sarcasms and delineations of character in some cases lost their force. Notably is this true of his religious impostors, his Tartuffes. Take for instance "Stiggins." Now, Stiggins had become already an impossible caricature long before the end of the last century. The Stigginses of that time, as of our own day, did not as a class, while preaching teetotalism, perpetually get drunk on rum-punch or anything else. Such crude form of hypocrisy, if it ever existed outside the caricatures of a novelist, had long since died out. The hypocrisy of this later period may be intrinsically no better than that of the "Stiggins" of **Pickwick**; on the contrary, it is worse, in so far as it is far more subtle and hence more dangerous. A pious "shepherd" like our old friend "Stiggins" is after all very easily found out, and when found out, his reputation inevitably collapses. Nobody would take up his defence. Things are different now. The pious Nonconformist preacher of our own day and the recent past still preaches abstinence, alcoholic and sexual, *anti*-gambling, and *anti* many other things, only not, of course, anti-moneymaking by the approved methods of capitalistic exploitation. The type of the modern Stiggins, the modern Tartuffe, is rather to be found in the Nonconformist divine who declaims against all the above sins in the pulpit and on the platform, and whose sincerity "moults no feather" (as Shakespeare has it) – in other words, who probably practises what he preaches in this respect. (At least there is no evidence that he does not do so.) But now comes the test. Our Nonconformist divine, who prides himself on devoutly exhorting- pillar as he is of the Nonconformist conscience – to *bourgeois* morality in all its hues, has influential friends connected with mining speculation in another continent. He acquires stock amounting perhaps to valuable holdings in their mining companies. It becomes the interest of the mining magnates to acquire the political control of the land in which their mines are situated, in order to obtain thereby greater freedom for the exploitation of mining labour. In consequence, the magnates in question, under cover of a patriotic cry, engineer a war for the conquest of the territory concerned and its annexation to Great Britain. What does our Non-conformist, pious and devout, zealous in seeking to save the normal non-ascetic human-non-ascetic, that is, in the points above referred to as the subject of his pulpit and platform diatribes – what does this gentleman (who, *bien entendu*, was accustomed, when he had everything to gain and nothing to lose by it, to plead the cause of peace and the freedom and independence of small and weak nationalities) – what, I say, does he do when it is a question of an aggressive war and the conquest and annexation of a numerically weak people in the interest of his friends, the mining magnates, and the enhancement of the value of his own holdings in the mines ? He champions the war, denounces its victims, and places himself unreservedly on the side of the mining war agitation of his friends, prepared to defend all the trickery, treachery, and lying involved in their wantonly provocative conduct. This man almost certainly never in his life got drunk on rum-punch or on any other alcoholic stimulant. On the contrary, he is reported to have drunk himself to death on tea, as befitted a pillar of the Nonconformist conscience and a leading light of total abstinence. No; our modern Stigginses and Tartuffes know a trick worth two of the rum-punch business, the red nose, and, for that matter, of sexual gallantries or other like peccadilloes abhorrent to the Nonconformist conscience and its votaries. Class interest and financial gain are more in their way than personal and private sins. This in an illustration of how Dickens and the early-Victorian novelists have lost already their savour and are likely to become pointless for future generations.

The question of the evolution of hypocrisy, as of roguery generally, is always interesting. The mediaeval fraudulent baker would stick a lump of clay or a stone in the middle of his loaf to make it weigh heavier. The modern fraudulent baker is better advised than to play such a clumsy trick. *He* makes his extra profit through cheapening his flour by adulteration, or otherwise lessening the cost of production, to the deterioration of the product. So the modern Stiggins scorns the methods of hypocrisy affected by his Dickensian prototype. The hypocrisy he so ably cultivates bears the impress of calculated thought and sober reflection. The above is, of course, only one instance of the way in which the wit and wisdom even of such a classic humorist in fiction as Charles Dickens has worn thin within a couple of generations. Many more could be given, such, for instance, as some of the pleasantries, and above all the Cockney speech of Sam Weller – the latter, of course, as has been often noticed, having become to some extent pointless and its funniness blunted to the present generation of Englishmen.

The like observations might be made as regards other novelists that delighted our fathers and mothers, and for that matter, ourselves also, in our early days, that is, those of us who are already beginning to take on the autumn tints of the "sere and yellow."

In Art, the declining nineteenth century expressed itself in what is known as *Decadence* in its various forms. The aesthetic movement proper, of which John Ruskin was regarded as the protagonist, and the extreme and more especially decadent forms of it which were represented by Oscar Wilde and his circle, were alike dominant at this time. For other decadents we have only to mention, in painting and designing, the names of Whistler and Aubrey Beardsley to recall a host of imitators. As for the (as we may term it) old legitimate aesthetic movement, as realized in the art of painting and designing, it was represented during the period in question, first and foremost by Burne-Jones, for life a close friend of William Morris, and by his disciple, Walter Crane, who carried on the artistic tradition of it till his death early in the year 1915. On the Continent, this line of artistic conception, in so far as it was not merely imitation, may be deemed to have been embodied in the works of Arnold Bocklin, the Swiss painter (1827-1901). There was considerable difference, no doubt, but the painting with the suggestion of decorative design in it which characterized the English movement is unmistakably present in the latter artist. The influence of this art in Central Europe is very marked indeed. There is a peculiar sweep of line of a scroll-character, eminently Bocklinian, which meets one continually in the more recent decorative art of the Germanic countries.

The cult of Decadence, as we may call it, in literature and pcetry, of which the Oscar Wilde group was the extreme wing, had a considerable vogue in the declining years of the nineteenth century, and traces of its effects may still be seen in the minds of the younger generation. The "Fleshly School," as it was termed, of Swinburne, with its offshoots, was countered by the "Idyllic School," as championed by Robert Buchanan, representing the older tradition in English poetry. Both were caricatured by Gilbert and Sullivan in *Patience*. The rapid development of *Decadence* in art issued in a morbid craving for, and striving after, mere *bizarrerie*. It mattered not whether a thing were beautiful or ugly, provided it were sufficiently bizarre. This decadent tendency run mad, when transferred from the sphere of literature and art to that of morals and manners, resulted, as is well known, in the downfall of Oscar Wilde himself. While giving full weight, however, to the decadent current in promoting unnatural proclivities in sex as in other matters, it must not be forgotten that the "Social Purity" movement so-called, led at that time by men like Stead and Price Hughes, may easily furnish the seed ground for such forms of erratic vice. In this connexion I cannot but recall what was told me by an eminent Egyptian judge, now holding a distinguished position on the mixed tribunal at Cairo. Speaking of Oriental literature, and especially of the **Arabian Nights**, he related to me how, in discussing the subject with a learned Mollah, he asked him what he thought of the gross licentiousness of much Mohammedan literature, and whether he could justify it. "Yes," replied the Mollah; "you see, the true believers, who were the authors of this literature, had to do with populations in which unnatural sexual vice was prevalent. Now, their aim was to provide a counteractive by lascivious descriptions and stories which excited the passions of men in the right direction, turning their lusts into the normal channel." Whether this pronouncement of the Mollah was historically accurate, and such was really the high moral purpose of the Islamic authors of erotic Eastern literature, may perhaps be doubted. But anyway, the contention itself has something to be said for it. You cannot suppress natural passion. The authors of Eastern literature, according to the Mollah, found a tendency for it to run into unnatural channels, and tried by their literary allurements to entice it back into natural ones. Conversely, promoters of the Social Purity campaign, in trying to cast stumbling-blocks moral and material in the way of the natural outlet of human passion, are pursuing a course which may well lead directly or indirectly to sexual perversion.

In Music, the cult of Decadence, although its first beginning may be traced as far back as the eighties, has reached what one may hope is its extreme development only in our own day. The eccentricities of Richard Strauss have been outdone recently by the senseless *bizarreries* of a Schönberg, and the madness of an Italian apostle of mere noise. At the end of the last century Wagner had entered fully into the appreciation of the English musical public. Very little was listened to or cared for in the direction of Opera that was not Wagner. In classical music Brahms still held the field with many, but everywhere the Wagnerian music-drama brought full houses. Shaw discoursed on Wagner in the columns of the **World**, and published the substance of his articles in his little volume **The Complete Wagnerite**. As regards Shaw, by the way, in connexion with Wagner – about the time of the first production of the *Meistersinger* in London, in June 1890, he called my attention to the curious fact that the main themes of the work were built up on the interval of the fourth. He and I were, during this period, joint musical critics of an evening paper. He wrote over the pseudonym "Corno di Bassetto," I over that of "Musigena." I had often occasion to be away on the Continent at this time, and I remember on this very occasion of the first introduction of the *Meistersinger* I had arrived home just in time to attend the performance, which fell to my department. This rather disgusted Shaw, who felt himself unduly cut out. The result was that as my frequent absence from London often threw my side of the work on Shaw, I thought it only fair to resign the whole to him. He, I believe, held it for a little time longer and then also resigned, presumably finding that the columns of the **World** gave him enough scope for the expression of his views on music, and that the pressure of other literary work absorbed more and more of his time.

In Philosophy, outside the still considerable though waning influence of Mill, and still more of Herbert Spencer, the so-called "young Hegelian" movement held the field. Thomas Hill Green, who died in the early eighties, was its protagonist at Oxford. The movement in question must not be regarded as a mere resuscitation of the philosophy of Hegel himself. It rather represented a rehabilitation and re-adaptation of the whole fundamental line of thought in German philosophy, which, though it ended with the old Hegelian school yet took its first origin from Kant. The movement produced a not inconsiderable philosophical literature in England and America. R.B. (now Lord) Haldane and his brother Dr. J.S. Haldane, especially the former, were zealous propagandists of the new departure in British philosophy. Indeed, perhaps the most notable production of the movement may be considered Lord Haldane's book, **The Pathway of Reality**, which dates, however, from much later, having been published in 1903. The general position of this school was the leading one in English philosophy until well into the present century; afterwards, at least in its original form, it succumbed to the assaults of criticism, and its basic positions began to be challenged by various cross-currents, perhaps the chief of which was the line of thought centring in Henri Bergson. Notwithstanding, however, its vulnerability to criticism in the older shapes in which it has been presented, the philosophical Idealism, embodied in the movement from Kant to Hegel, unquestionably contains a fundamental element of truth which all future philosophical speculation will have to take account as basal.

In 1882 I contributed my own quota to the dominant philosophical interest by my translation of Kant's **Prolegomena** and **Metaphysical Foundations of Natural Science**, preceded by a short biography of Kant, published in Bohn's "Philosophical Library"; and, three years later, by my **Handbook to the History of Philosophy** in the same series. The Aristotelian Society was founded in 1881 by a small hand of independent students of philosophy, with the late Dr. Shadworth Hodgson as president. In its early years, as I remember it, it had not yet become so much the haunt of academic dignitaries, men of the chair, as it did at a later period.

In History, especially the history of institutions, the century-end showed some remarkable achievements. Freeman was still writing at the beginning of the nineties, and he, in conjunction with J.R. Green (then recently deceased), and Canon Stubbs were the leading lights in the new views of historical research as applied to English history. Green's **Short History of the English People**, which originally appeared in 1874, achieved enormous success, and was read by every Englishman and Englishwoman with any pretence to education during the last two decades of the nineteenth century. **Stubbs' Constitutional History**, though appealing to a more restricted class, had an almost equal success on its own lines. The most remarkable work in general history in this country produced by the declining nineteenth century may fairly be said to be the late Thomas Hodgkin's **Italy and Her Invaders**, the separate appearance of the eight volumes of which extended from 1880 to 1899, Hodgkin belonged to the same school as the historians above mentioned, and his work undoubtedly contains the most complete and exhaustive history of the "Barbarian invasions" that has ever been written in any language. One rises from a perusal of Hodgkin with the conviction that, as regards actual historical fact, at least, the last word has been said on this great subject. Covering as it does the ground of a considerable part of Gibbons' work, **Italy and Her Invaders** is a striking object-lesson in the advance of historical scholarship during the nineteenth century.

Talking of historical scholarship, it is a curious thing to notice how one occasionally finds a man of undoubted ability and real scholarship, who will be once in a way caught tripping in the most elementary fashion, within the bounds of the special subject to which he has devoted perhaps the greater part of his life. Thus, I believe it was the late Mr. F.J. Furnivall – and if any one was an adept in English Elizabethan literature certainly he was – who, on one occasion, in a review, made the outrageous *gaffe* of criticizing a preface by Ben Jonson to some contemporary author as if it had been the production of a modern editor. A more recent instance, not so flagrant as this, but showing at least a singular ignorance or lapse of memory as regards well-known historical source, came under lily notice in connexion with the eminent classical scholar and authority in Roman History, Professor Ferrero, of Turin. Conversing on various points relating to the civil wars at the end of the Republic, I mentioned a well-known passage in Plutarch's **Life of Sylla,** in which the story is told with considerable detail of a satyr or faun captured by the soldiery and brought to Sylla. I asked Professor Ferrero what he thought it meant. He, however, while hazarding the opinion that it possibly referred to some cretin, almost animal-like in appearance, such as are to be found in some mountainous districts, notably the Val d'Aosta, at this day, stated that he was quite unaware of the existence of the passage in question! And yet perhaps Professor Ferrero knows the sources of Roman history in general better than any other man living. May we take this as showing that the greatest scholars and the greatest specialists may be fallible even as other men – fallible, too, on elementary matters concerning their own specialism?

But even more than in the domain of general historical research is the period of the declining years of the nineteenth century signalized by the remarkable work done in connexion with the early history of institutions, together with Comparative Mythology and the science of Anthropology generally. As in history, so here, English scholars received a vast amount of assistance from, and were powerfully influenced by, continental, and especially German, scholarship. But there was also much original work done by English writers, besides the collection of material and its presentation as a coherent whole of theory. Asked to name the most striking contribution to human knowledge in the departments above mentioned, I think there are few competent to judge who would not give the palm to that remarkable book **The Golden Bough** of Professor (now Sir James) Frazer, of Cambridge, of which the first edition was published in 1890, and new editions, each with large additions of fresh matter, have been constantly appearing since. This great work has produced, in many respects, a revolution in our views of primitive society and of the early periods of universal history. Valuable work was also done by other writers, but none of quite so much originality as that of Frazer.[1]

Among works dealing with anthropological studies from another side may be mentioned Morgan's **Ancient Society**, which Karl Marx was one of the first to appreciate on its appearance in 1876. But it did not receive general recognition till the century was nearing its close. The works of Von Maurer and Maine, belonging to the period of the mid-century or a little later, formed the groundwork for much of the research into the beginnings of social history during the time of which we are speaking.

As before remarked, the early eighties marked the climax of a great change in the intellectual life of England. It was then that the advent of a new generation made itself very distinctly felt. The difference, for instance, between the England of the

58

sixties and the England of the eighties, is immense as regards the relative culture of the two periods alike in respect of its depth and extension. In the sixties an independent all-round intellectual life was strictly limited to a section, of the academic, literary, and scientific classes, and even here the outlook was as a rule very narrow compared with what it became a couple of decades afterwards. The social strata affected by intellectual interests showed an enormous advance in the later as compared with the earlier period. Middle-class households, where in the sixties antimacassars, wax-flowers, on the walls, religious texts worked in Berlin wool, sentimental drawing-room songs, cheap dance music or transcription of banal Italian opera airs lying on a chair beside the piano, religious books alternating with cheap novels in the bookcase, Martin Tupper's **Proverbial Philosophy**, and, as the nearest approach to actual literature, Longfellow's poems, on the drawing-room table – domestic establishments such as these gradually disappeared in the interval between the two periods. The generation which came to its own in the eighties had acquired truer instincts and higher interests in art, literature, music, and the deeper problems of life, individual and social, than its predecessors of the early- and mid-Victorian period The penetration of what is known as the "higher culture" into the ranks of the working classes proper followed some years later. It is noteworthy in this connexion that the Socialism of the eighties and even the early nineties – i.e. the new scientific Socialism of Marx and all that that implied – was mainly a middle-class movement. The working classes, to whom in the nature of things the movement ought to have appealed, were largely apathetic and unresponsive in this country for a long time. The work of education in the new social and economic views was mainly done by middle-class men. So it was generally. The new intellectual life of the country began to affect the bulk of the working classes in England hardly before the late nineties. Progress has been taking place, of course, ever since, but it is not amiss to recall the fact that the starting-point of much of our subsequent advance dates from the last twenty years of the nineteenth century and the new intellectual life which grew up during that time.

In the present chapter I have only attempted to call attention to some of the leading features in the literature, art, and science of the period in question. The picture here outlined can be readily filled up by all who will. Those days do not lie long behind us in reality, but the strain and stress of modern life have had a tendency to alter our perspective of events and periods, and already this nineteenth century-end begins to wear the aspect of history, and to seem more remote from us than its actual distance in time would warrant.

## Note

1. Talking of the **Golden Bough**, an incident occurred quite recently, illustrating at once the increase of education and intelligence in the English working classes of the present day as compared with the last generation, and the wide social range of the celebrity attained by this famous book. A window-cleaner coming one morning to perform his functions, and seeing a copy of one of the volumes of the **Golden Bough** lying open on my study table, observed to one of the household, with much apparent interest, pointing to the open page, "Ah, that's a very remarkable book, ma'am – a very remarkable book!"

# IV. The Social-Democratic Federation

IN the late seventies and the early eighties the workman's club was a strong political force in the land. This was especially the case as regards London, where there was a considerable and well-organized network of these clubs throughout the whole metropolis. At this time the workman's club movement on its political side was not much more than a wing of the official Liberal party. There was little or no political initiative or influence of ideas outside the range of current political questions and party politics in any of them. The leading political workman's club in London was the "Eleusis Club," Chelsea, the constituency for which the late Sir Charles Dilke at that time sat. But there was not a district throughout the metropolis that did not boast of one or more of them, though of course they varied much in size and influence. Now it occurred to the, at that time, independent Radical, Henry Mayers Hyndman, early in 1881, to endeavour to weld the best elements in these clubs into an independent and coherent political party, under the name of the "Democratic Federation." The principles on which it was to be based were unpretentious enough at first glance, but Hyndman, who, as we have seen, had come into contact with Marx, had the foundation of a British Socialist party already in view. The preliminary meeting was held and the organization founded in the early Spring of 1881. At its inauguration there were some persons associated with it, such, for instance, as the late Butler Johnstone, who, as its aims became more closely defined, dropped out. But the organization continued, small and unpretentious as it was, notwithstanding, though it never achieved altogether its original ostensible aim, namely that of uniting in one solid phalanx the Radical workmen's clubs of the metropolis. Speaking of myself, I made the acquaintance of Hyndman in 1882, and the same year joined the "Democratic Federation." At this time the Irish agrarian question and the Land League were very much to the fore, and the new organization was largely occupied with matters connected with the Irish agitation.

The offices of the Democratic Federation were at 9 Palace Chambers, Westminster, opposite the Houses of Parliament, and here in February and March 1883 a series of conferences were held on certain pressing questions of the day, which subsequently became crystallized under the name of "steppingstones" (to Socialism) in the practical programme of the organization. At the same time new and important recruits came in, who infused fresh life into the movement and enabled Hyndman to give it a definite Socialist direction. These were J.L. Joynes, who had just resigned his mastership at Eton; H.H. Champion, the son of the late General Champion, an Army officer, who had given up his commission, disgusted with the Egyptian War of 1882; Harry Quelch, then a journeyman packer in Cannon Street; John Burns, who, if I remember rightly, joined a few months later, and William Morris. The present writer also, now that the movement was becoming more definitively Socialist, began to take a more active interest in it than heretofore. During the Summer of 1883 much propaganda work was done in the open air. In the late Autumn of that year I joined the executive committee of the Democratic Federation. About the same time the donation of £300 from the well-known poet and writer on Social subjects, Edward Carpenter, towards the founding of a weekly organ for the new body, led to arrangements being made for the starting of the paper **Justice** in January of the year 1884. The first editor was an Irishman, an ex-military man named Fitzgerald, who had been war correspondent for English newspapers in the Russo-Turkish campaign of 1877-8, and who claimed to be a great authority on affairs of the Near East. This good man, I may remark parenthetically, some ten years later seems to have come to a mysterious and premature end. Having again taken up his old *métier* of journalist-correspondent, he went out to Greece, where he married the daughter of the French Consul at Corinth. While on a journalistic tour into Thessaly and other parts of the Balkan peninsula, all trace of him was lost, and he was never heard of again. The presumption was that he had been murdered by Turks. Austria and Turkey, it may be mentioned, were always his especial *bêtes noires*. To come back to **Justice**. Our friend Fitzgerald not proving the ideal editor, Hyndman undertook the editorship himself. We all collaborated in the endeavour to make the journal a success Hyndman, Joynes, Champion, the Austrian revolutionary Andreas Scheu, and the present writer used to work regularly for it. Morris, who had by this time thrown himself enthusiastically into the movement, contributed his well-known poem *All for the Cause* to the first number, and afterwards other poems and articles. I well remember how, at the annual conference of the Democratic Federation in the Spring of the previous year, I successfully exercised my arts of persuasion in inducing Morris, whom I had recently come to know, to join the executive council of the new party, he having refused when first proposed. But of Morris I shall have occasion to speak more fully later.

The Summer of 1884 showed a vastly increased activity in the ranks of the SDF. This activity took various forms. Besides the getting out of the paper **Justice** week by week, the publication and distribution, often at the corners of the streets, of leaflets and other propagandist literature, added to the: preaching of Socialism in the open air, kept the leading members of the organization sufficiently busy. The last-mentioned means of serving the cause resulted in frequent collisions with the police authorities on the ostensible ground of "obstruction." But, however, that this was merely the ostensible and not the real ground was proved by the fact that itinerant preachers of the orthodox Christian sects and teetotal advocates were not interfered with. The obstruction of traffic only existed, or at least only became a public nuisance, where Socialist orators were concerned. This interference at last reached such a point that in the interests of the right of free speech and public meetings in the open air, the Radical and workmen's clubs of London took the matter up. Things culminated in what was known at the time as the "Dod Street victory." Members of the Democratic Federation having been summoned for technical "obstruction" on successive Sunday mornings at a space in Dod Street where no foot or vehicular traffic was really interfered with, it was decided to make a definitive stand. Accordingly, in conjunction with the Radical Associations and the workmen's clubs of the metropolis a great demonstration was organized. This took place one fine Sunday morning, when a procession of some forty thousand people marched to Dod Street for the purpose of holding a mass meeting. Before this imposing demonstration the local police Jacks-in-office had to give way. The meeting was successfully held and addressed by all the well-known political Democrats of London, in addition to the Socialist members of the Democratic Federation. From that time forward the persecution of the speakers at Socialist meetings became less frequent.

Towards the end of the Summer of 1884 two currents of opinion became manifest on the executive council of the Federation. The annual congress of the body was held in August in one of the larger meeting-rooms of Palace Chambers, Westminster. At this meeting the name Democratic Federation was changed to that of Social Democratic Federation. In the council elected on this occasion it was that the differences spoken of later on arose. Personal questions undoubtedly played their part, but there were conflicting opinions also upon matters of tactics – on the one side were Hyndman, Burns, Williams, Quelch, Fitzgerald, then acting as secretary of the body, and Champion, who were supposed to be anxious to subordinate the propaganda of Socialist principle to the urging forward of immediate practical aims in politics by the ordinary political methods. Such was at least the view of their aims taken by Morris, Scheu, Eleanor Marx (the daughter of Karl Marx), who had been elected on to the council at the August conference, myself, and others, who were desirous of pushing a purely Socialist propaganda without regard to the expediencies or exigencies of practical politics, and without wasting time (which might be better employed, it was thought) with the methods and aims of the political life of the moment. This as nearly as possible represents, I should say, the main theoretical difference between the two tendencies on the executive council of the SDF (as it was now becoming the custom to abbreviate the full name), which culminated in the "split" in the body that took place at the end of the year and the foundation of the Socialist League early in January 1885. There were of course, as before said, personal friction, suspicion, and mistrust, such as are always engendered on similar occasions. How unjust some of this suspicion was, the subsequent course of events has shown. For example, the notion that Hyndman ever had in him the nature of a time-serving politician, capable of subordinating convictions to the chances of a political career, seems now too absurd for words. Not to speak of his sacrifice of political success on the ordinary lines to his general Socialist convictions, it is in part, at least, thanks to his rigidly uncompromising attitude on every point of political and economic principle that he is not at the time of writing a member of the House of Commons. The "split" was unfortunate from many points of view, not only from that of the regrettable personal differences it engendered between individuals, and which it took some years to compose, but also from that of the Socialist cause, the progress of which it undoubtedly headed back for a while, although not so much as might have been expected. As time showed, the excuse or reason for the rupture, so far as its theoretical grounds were concerned, was utterly inadequate. The divergence, in matters of tactics and political policy, was not nearly so wide or important as many of the withdrawing section imagined. Looking back at the events of the time, it is impossible to resist the conclusion that the personal element – differences of temperament and ways of looking at things, even where fundamental convictions were held in common – leading to the mistrust and suspicion above referred to, suspicion fostered by mischief-makers, was largely at the back of the secession.

The last meeting of the old council of the SDF, which

finally determined the breach, and which took place in a room rented as offices by the body in the basement of Palace Chambers, Westminster, on the evening of the 24th of December 1884, was of a dramatic character. Mrs. (afterwards Lady), Burne-Jones on hearing Morris's description of it the next day, said it reminded her of one of the scenes in Turgenieff's novel **Smoke**, in which was depicted the coming together of a Russian secret political society. There was a full attendance of members of the council, eighteen in all, who sat round the centre table. The rest of the room was crowded with partisans of either side. All the members of the council made speeches in their turn, their points being greeted by vociferous demonstrations of approval and disapproval. Various incidents took place. The debate was on a vote of censure on Hyndman as regards his political attitude and conduct in connexion with the affairs of the Federation. On the vote being taken, the result was ten for, and eight against, the motion; the names including: for the resolutionWilliam Morris, Robert Banner, Andreas Sheu, Edward Aveling, Eleanor Marx Aveling, myself; and against the resolution – H.M. Hyndman, H. H. Champion, J. C. Frost, John E. Williams, Henry Quelch, John Burns, etc.

Though, as will be seen, the supporters of the resolution were in a slight numerical majority, nevertheless immediately it was passed they declared their own resignation from the body. This somewhat erratic proceeding was due to the fact that Morris objected to himself and his followers, who backed the resolution, remaining in the body under conditions which he felt would inevitably lead to a continuance of violent controversy and personal recrimination. The matter had been discussed at a meeting of the seceding section held the day before the council meeting. Morris, after strongly urging this point of view, succeeded in carrying it, and exacting pledges from all his supporters to follow the course of action he proposed. Accordingly, the somewhat anomalous procedure was witnessed of the majority of a council resigning, to leave the organization it represented in the hands of the defeated minority. But the seceders, notwithstanding their abandonment of the original organization, had no intention of abandoning work for Socialism.

The result of the secession from the SDF was the foundation, a few days later, at the beginning of January 1885, of the Socialist League under the auspices of William Morris. The manifesto of the new League, expounding in brief the principles of Socialism on which it was founded, was drawn up by William Morris and myself on the New Year's Eve. Offices were taken for the organization in the upper story of a building in Farringdon Road, a new paper appearing as the organ of the League, for the first year monthly, but afterwards weekly, to which, at Morris's suggestion, was given the name of **The Commonweal**. The basis of the new organization rigidly excluded anything of the nature of immediate political action, such as the taking part in electoral contests, whether parliamentary or local. The principle of the League was to be, for an indefinite time at least, purely educational, though the belief in the comparative nearness of a cataclysmic social revolution loomed in the background in the minds of many. The idea implicit in not a few of those who belonged to the Socialist League was more or less that of a federation of Socialist societies throughout the country, bearing some sort of analogy to the federated Jacobin Clubs of the French Revolution, which should educate and organize public opinion, especially of the working classes, so that when the cataclysm to which the capitalist system was leading up should supervene, these societies might be in a position to give direction to the revolutionary movement. But as things turned out, this total abandonment of all political and practical action generally on the part of the League had untoward consequences, to which the organization itself finally succumbed after an existence of some seven years. Nevertheless, for the first two or three years from its foundation the Socialist League undoubtedly did much fruitful work in the direction of Socialist propaganda. Meetings were held in halls and in the open air, leaflets and pamphlets were published, including manifestos on important current events, such as the Home Rule question, the Soudan War, the war in Burmah, etc. **The Commonweal**, to which Morris and the present writer regularly contributed, also did well for the first two or three years. Some of Morris's poems, subsequently published separately, first appeared in **The Commonweal**. A selection of his political articles, written at this time, might be worth republishing in book-form, as likely to be interesting to his many admirers. I continued to assist Morris in the editorship of **The Commonweal** till the Summer of 1888, when, owing to reasons which will directly be made clear, I resigned from the League, though without any breach in my personal friendship with Morris.

Certain untoward consequences resulting, in a great measure, from the strictly anti-political action principles of the League have been already spoken of. These consequences were not long in showing themselves, though it took some two or three years for them to develop to a marked extent. The attitude in question of the League, combined with a certain want of precision in the definition of its theoretical principles on certain sides, left the door open for the intrusion of doubtful elements of an anarchistic character. These elements grew stronger as time went on, and found support in a certain side of Morris's own temperament. The result was as might have been foreseen. The Socialist League became impossible for those who wished to see it grow up into a strong party organization for the propagation of the principles of scientific Socialism, and if not immediately, at least later on, definitely to take part in political action of some kind. The great bulk of those who thought thus in the League resigned, in this way leaving the body in the hands of a rump consisting of Anarchists and Semi-anarchists, with a few others who did not formally resign for fear of hurting Morris's feelings. The further history of the League was a record of internal disputes and failure to achieve anything towards the ostensible objects for which the organization had been founded. Morris struggled manfully with adversity for a time, but finding those associated with him impossible to work with from any point of view, gradually lost heart, and ultimately, in the Summer of 1889, himself withdrew from the now rapidly disintegrating section of the Socialist movement he had himself founded, followed by the few personal friends who had continued with him. As may be imagined, the remains of the body soon after this fell to pieces, the **Commonweal** went under, and the Socialist League even in name ceased to exist.

Though the original secession from the Social Democratic Federation was an unquestionable mistake, yet the mistake having been made, the foundation of the Socialist League and the work he put into it reflects the highest credit on Morris personally. Kudos he had enough already in other directions, and financially the maintenance of the movement and all that appertained thereto was a heavy drain upon his time and purse. Altogether, a more personally disinterested man in his public work never existed.

There are two public incidents that occurred during the existence of the League which should not be passed over without mention. The first was the great London riot on the 8th of February 1886. The story of this riot is well known. A meeting was called for the afternoon of that day, a Monday, in Trafalgar Square, to discuss the question of "fair trade" and "sugar bounties." There being much unemployment at the time, Trafalgar Square became crowded, long before the hour announced for the meeting, by numbers of hungry, workless men who found in the event a means of distraction. The opportunity was taken, alike by speakers of the Federation and the League, to point out the futility of nostrums such as the "fair trade" and "sugar bounties" agitation, and to urge the claims of Socialist reorganization as the only cure for the evils of the present system, with its recurrent crises, in which large sections of the working classes are thrown upon the pavement. Some of the speeches made were strong in their language. One of the League speakers delivered himself of an oration in which the words "lead" and "bread" appeared in antithetical juxtaposition, in suchwise, it was alleged, as amounted to an incitement to violence. However this may have been, the promoters of the meeting, finding themselves outwitted by the Socialist agitators, peremptorily closed the proceedings, which were beginning to become disorderly. Meanwhile, it was proposed by the SDF speakers, to the crowd, to march through the West End to Hyde Park, there to hold another meeting on the question of unemployment. Accordingly, some eight or ten thousand persons, headed by H.M. Hyndman, H.H. Champion, John Burns, and John E. Williams, advanced in the direction of Pall Mall. There rioting began, the immediate causes of which were variously stated, and continued along the route to Hyde Park. A somewhat uproarious meeting was held in the Park, after which the rioters dispersed eastwards in straggling bands, looting shops on the way.

The affair, as might be expected, caused an enormous sensation at the time. The newspapers were full of it for days afterwards. There was a perfect panic: the "Mansion House Fund for the Unemployed" jumped up in a day or two from £3,000 to £75,000. Such was the terror of the wealthy classes at the new danger that they imagined threatened them! The incident had its upshot in the prosecution of Hyndman, Champion, Burns, and Williams on a charge of sedition. Resulting circumstances brought the personalities of the League and the Federation much closer together than heretofore. One of the papers published an alleged interview with Morris in which he was made to blame the conduct of our SDF friends as the cause of the riots. He promptly wrote protesting against having said anything of the kind. At the same time, while exonerating the SDF leaders from all responsibility as to having had any share in causing the riots, he expressed the opinion that the latter had not been without their uses in opening the eyes of the middle and upper classes to the realities of things. The trial resulted in the acquittal of all four of the accused. Singularly enough, the man who seemed nearest to conviction on account of his alleged utterances was the since so moderate Liberal politician, John Burns. This was partly owing to the attribution to him by the Prosecution of a speech he had never made, to wit, that anent "bread" and "lead." The result of the prosecution was a distinct fiasco for the Government, and the whole affair of the riots, from beginning to end, was a tremendous advertisement for Socialism, especially the SDF. The incident certainly brought home the social problem, in a manner which probably nothing else would have done, to the average mind of : he middle and upper classes. The circumstances attending the riots also called the attention of the working classes to the fact that Socialism offered a solution of the social problem.

The second of the events referred to was the disturbances in connexion with the proclaimed meeting in Trafalgar Square on November 21st of the next year, 1887. After the riots of February 1886, during the panic following them, the Chief of the Police, Sir Edmund Henderson, resigned as having failed to cope with the exigencies of the situation. In his place came an Army man, Sir Charles Warren, whose aim evidently was to pose in the role of a Saviour of Society and as a person of great determination of character. He decreed, accordingly, the closing of Trafalgar Square for public meetings. The matter was brought to a test by the announcement, on the part of the Irish party, the Radicals, and the Socialists of the metropolis, of a mass meeting to be held in Trafalgar Square on Sunday, 21st of November 1887, to discuss the Irish matters which were then uppermost in the general interest of the public. The unemployed question being still acute and likely to be heard of at the meeting, also the fact that one of the main objects of its promoters was to test the question of the right of assembly in Trafalgar Square, the situation was an interesting, not to say a threatening one. The police were in strong force and the military behind. As the contingents of the various Radical clubs, branches of the Socialist organizations, and Irish Societies of London debouched through the streets leading into the Square, they were attacked and mostly dispersed

71

by the police. Many persons were injured in scuffles with the constabulary, and one man. John Linnell, was killed and had a public funeral the following Sunday. The whole affair created almost as much sensation as the riots of twenty months previously. I was myself away in Zürich at the time. What gave a special interest to this event was the effect it had upon Morris's views. Up to this time he had more or less believed in the possible success of a revolutionary outbreak on the part of the populace of our great cities – a revolutionary outbreak in the old style of the French Revolution, of Paris in July 1830, or the June days of 1848. But Morris, who headed the contingent furnished by the Socialist League on this occasion, lost all his confidence as to the power of an unorganized or imperfectly organized crowd to offer an effective resistance to the forces of the modern State. So far at least as England was concerned, whether rightly or wrongly, the occurrences of this day seemed to have practically settled the matter for him. He wrote me a letter immediately afterwards to this effect, telling me that he had always recognized the probability of any scratch body of men getting the worst of it in a rough-and-tumble with the police, not to speak of the military, yet he had not realized till that day how soon such a body could be scattered by a comparatively small but well-organized force. Later on, when I had come back to London, he vividly described to me how, singly and in twos and threes, his followers began for a few moments to make a show of fight with the police, and how in vain he tried to rally, them to effect a determined dash as a united body on their goal, namely, Trafalgar Square itself. The whole affair, he said, was over in scarcely more than three or four minutes. This incident certainly had a strong effect in making Morris pessimistic as to the success of any popular civil rising under existing circumstances, however just might be the cause in which it was undertaken.

Before leaving the subject of the Social Democratic Federation and Socialist League, I may recall an amusing incident which occurred in connexion with the Croydon branch of the former body, as illustrating the value sometimes to be attached to a crowd's manifestations of sympathy or antipathy at a meeting. Our Croydon friends were in the habit of holding Socialist meetings on fine Sunday afternoons during the Summer on an open space called Duppas Hill. Some young men of the small clerk and shopman type were incited by paid agents of the Tory party to interrupt speakers and disturb the meetings. This went on for two or three Sundays in succession, when our friends, who had succeeded in getting the addresses of these agents, bethought themselves of negotiating with them. Accordingly, they called upon the leader and offered him for the next Sunday two shillings a head for his men to keep order, in place of the eighteen-pence he admitted he had been receiving from the Tories to create disturbance. Result: the following Sunday consternation for the knot of youths of the small clerk and shopman type, who found their sport spoilt and their persons threatened by their whilom friends and encouragers! During the ensuing week the leader of the provocative agents, who by the way was a professional pugilist, succeeded in inducing the Tories to raise their price to half-a-crown a head for his future services to their cause. The following Sunday therefore found things again as they were before. In view of the situation, the finances of the branch not admitting of its being "raised" in this way sixpence per head per week indefinitely, and also as the time of year for open-air meetings was nearly over, our friends decided to discontinue the gatherings for that season, although the pugilist leader intimated that he was still open to an offer from their side.

The history of the SDF after the collapse of the Socialist League need not detain us in detail. Many of those who had been connected with the League since its foundation, including myself, who had, as already stated, resigned from the body in 1888, after it became clear that the anarchistic and quasi-anarchistic elements were getting the upper hand, had already rejoined the Social Democratic Federation before the League finally broke up. The original body now became for some years the only Socialist organization in the country. Speaking of my own revived connexion with it, I was soon re-elected to the London Executive Council, and for a short time in 1892 took over the editorship of **Justice**, which Hyndman, owing to the pressure of other work, had been compelled to abandon. I was myself obliged to retire before very long, owing to the fact that family calls gave occasion for my absence from England at this time for some months during the year. Henry Quelch was then appointed editor at a regular salary, which, comparatively small though it was, especially at first, enabled him to give up all other work and devote himself entirely to the paper and the organization it represented. The efficiency and laborious energy he put into his new occupations from the beginning continued till his death in 1913, a period of over twenty years. The Social Democratic Federation maintained its activity under that name till 1911. For some time before this a feeling had grown up within the body for enlarging (as it was deemed) the scope of the influence of the old organization.

The Independent Labour Party, which was started early in 1893 as a working-class political organization independent of the two traditional political parties in the State, though at first founded on a non-Socialist basis, in a few years became permeated with Socialist ideas (albeit in many cases of a somewhat nebulous character), and before long openly declared itself Socialist. It thenceforward tended to absorb most of the vague floating Socialist aspiration of the country. About the same time as the Independent Labour Party came into existence, Robert Blatchford, with a small circle of collaborators and sympathizers, started his weekly paper, **The Clarion**, in which most of the main principles of Socialism found expression in a popular form. The **Clarion** had considerable influence throughout the country, societies of its supporters, calling themselves "Clarionets," being founded in many of the larger towns. But the influence alike of the independent Labour Party and of the **Clarion** and its devotees was largely in the provincial centres of the Midlands and the

North, especially the latter. In London and the South of England the SDF still held the field. Now, the desire on the part of its members to acquire a largely increased influence in the industrial districts of northern and central Britain induced them to give ear to the promptings of Victor Grayson (the elect of Colne Valley in 1908) and others, to merge the SDF in a larger national party, it being represented that the SDF would never make appreciable further progress under its old name, having acquired an evil reputation throughout the country for narrow sectarianism. This meant presumably that it was too little time-serving in its policy, and that its adhesion to Socialist principle was too strict. Be this as it may, a resolution to change the name of "Social Democratic Federation" to that of "British Socialist Party" was passed at the conference of the year 1911. The result hardly justified the expectations which led to the surrender of the original name, honoured as it was by well-nigh a generation of hard uphill work in the propaganda of Socialist principles, and in the endeavour to make Socialism a political force in the country At first a few Independent Labour men, "Clarionets," and some hitherto unattached Socialists joined the rechristened organization, but most of these outside elements soon fell away, so that the new "British Socialist Party" before long became, as regards membership, practically identical with the old "Social Democratic Federation," the change of name having had no appreciable effect one way or the other on its numbers or influence. The general history of the organization since it was reconstituted as the British Socialist Party belongs more to the region of current events than to that of reminiscences, and hence need not detain us here.

The general progress of Socialist ideas in this country within recent years is by no means commensurable with the membership of any definitely organized Socialist body. The whole of modern Democratic thought is more or less permeated with Socialist ideas and aspirations. The administrative changes to which the European War has given rise have educated the public opinion of the working classes, on more than one side of elementary economic reconstruction, in a Socialist direction. The apparent temporary eclipse on the political side of the old principle of Internationalism, the substitution even for the moment of the struggle of races in place of the struggle of classes, is, I am convinced, far more superficial and far more temporary than many would have us believe. In this respect the Great War will undoubtedly be found to have cut both ways. While on one side it will have tended to inter-racial estrangement, on another side it will have tended equally to effect an advance in race-solidarity. But it is not to be doubted that in the long run, and with the resumption of the class-struggle in its full intensity, all estrangement, all race-prejudice, will before very long disappear in face of the rise of a new International, which the working classes of the civilized world, taught by the experience of the past, will raise to a strength and influence in the determining of inter-racial disputes (mainly interesting as they are to the dominant classes of the countries concerned) such as will render any renewal of the great race struggles of the past for ever more impossible. With the firm establishment and corresponding influence of such a new International the United States of Europe, hitherto regarded as a utopian dream, will be, if not at once realized, in a fair way towards realization.

As to the ideal side of Socialism, the decline in effectiveness of the old objects of religious sentiment and in the theoretical basis generally of what I have elsewhere termed "introspective" Ethics and Religion, through the universal collapse of a living and active faith in the Supernatural and its sanctions, together with the accompanying equally universal spread of an "agnostic" attitude of mind towards all dogmatic creeds based thereupon, has opened the way for the definite substitution of a human and social ideal, and of human and social sanctions, for the old theological ones. The definite acceptance of Socialism, with all that it connotes in its ulterior consequences, unconsciously serves to fill a place in men's minds formerly occupied by the various creeds outworn. Thus does the conception of Human Brotherhood and Unity, as expressed in the old Trinity of the French Revolution – Liberty, Equality, and Fraternity – acquire alike a new and definite meaning in itself and a fresh significance as the object of religious sentiment, The economic reconstruction which is the material basis of Socialism, and which is often taken to be the whole of Socialism, will, with the growth alike in diffusion and in intensity of the new meaning and implications involved in human destiny, be seen in its true proportions. While the politico-economic revolution in the organization of Society will be more than ever before recognized as the first and indispensable condition of all higher social life, whether in thought, in art, or in conduct, the Socialist ideal will be seen not to be limited to this mere politico-economic change, but to reach forward to something above and beyond any mere material transformation.

# V. Personalities of the Socialist Movement in England

THE first place in any characterization of the individuals who have played a part in the Socialist movement in Great Britain must be given to the man who is in every way the founder of that movement, Henry Mayers Hyndman. I first became acquainted with Hyndman in 1882. He was then living in Devonshire Street, Portland Place, and was regarded generally by Liberals and orthodox Radicals as an eccentric political freelance who was working in the Tory interests. This was largely owing to the fact that he had strongly opposed the Russophile agitation of Gladstone from 1876 to 1878, during the crisis which led up to the Russo-Turkish War, and during the war itself. His pro-Turkish and anti-Russian views on the war had naturally thrown him into contact with the Tory party and with Beaconsfield, at that time its leader. His relations with Beaconsfield, Salisbury, and other Tory celebrities will be found given in detail in his two autobiographical volumes entitled respectively **The Record of an Adventurous Life** and **More Reminiscences**. Another circumstance which led with some enthusiastic Radicals to suspicions as to the thorough-going character of Hyndman's democratic sentiments was that at the preliminary meeting at which the Democratic Federation was founded in the Spring of 1881, over which he presided, he had opposed a motion to place the immediate abolition of the monarchy on the practical programme of the Federation. This was imagined at the time by some of those present to be an expression of Tory respectability and loyalty to the throne. It was really nothing of the kind, but simply due to a desire not to encumber the new platform with "planks" for the time being inexpedient. The old Dilke Republican agitation of the seventies had comparatively recently "petered out" from lack of public interest. As a matter of fact, a year or two later, opposition in principle to all monarchical forms of government was inserted with Hyndman's full approval as one of the objects of the organization, though not on its programme for immediate agitation. It must not be forgotten, moreover, that the Democratic Federation was not founded at first as a Socialist body, but with the object of uniting the Radical and workmen's clubs of London, first of all on a general Democratic programme wide enough, if possible, to include them all.

At the time I speak of, Hyndman was not merely the prime mover and the director of the affairs of the new organization founded under his auspices, but also its chief financier. Heavy pecuniary losses subsequently disabled him from continuing this assistance, but it lasted long enough to place the Democratic Federation on a sufficiently stable footing to attract important new recruits, among them William Morris, also a man of means, whose financial assistance for a year or two subsequently, that is, until the "split," was timely and valuable.

The special characteristic of Hyndman has always been his perennial buoyancy of temperament. Throughout all his career one hardly ever found Hyndman downhearted. Many have laughed at the expression so often heard from him in the early eighties, "things are getting hot," an expression used at a time when there were little or no signs of revolutionary perturbation, outside the local question of Ireland, on the political horizon. It was all that the Socialist advocate could do to raise a small section of the working classes out of their apathy to take any interest whatever in their position and in the means to the attainment of a state of society in which they should cease to be mere wage drudges. But his very buoyancy of disposition, which saw things moving much faster than they were doing in reality, undoubtedly helped to sustain the flagging energies of many of Hyndman's followers in the Federation. Indeed, some thought that these expressions of confidence in the rapid progress of the elements of disruption in our capitalist society, as in the mental preparedness of the masses for social reorganization, were made with express calculation for the purpose of encouragement. I do not think, however, this, if at all, was more than partially the case. Hyndman's optimism was undoubtedly the result of his natural temperament, and a very desirable temperament it is for one engaged in the uphill work involved in the advocacy of an unpopular cause, or at least a cause towards which the mass of men are for the time being apathetic. The "never say die" attitude which takes no discouragement is certainly one of the most striking characteristics of the man Hyndman alike in connexion with public and private affairs.

Hyndman's sincere enthusiasm for the cause to which he has so zealously devoted his life is in nothing more crucially exhibited than in his conduct after the "split" had deprived the SDF of Morris's financial assistance and of many workers on its behalf. He ranged himself alongside of the proletarians of the organization, not only in open-air speaking in the parks and elsewhere, but even in the selling of Socialist literature along Fleet Street and the Strand. This reminds me of one of Hyndman's traits that has often been the subject of jest and animadversion among the profane. I allude to his partiality for the frock-coat, the pot-hat, and the linked shirt-cuff. It was in this garb that he was on more than one occasion to be seen selling **Justice** in the thoroughfares named. Now, speaking personally, nothing would induce me to don this to me hideous and sordid uniform of the capitalist era. But then I suppose I should be termed Bohemian in such matters. There is, however, nothing of the Bohemian in the usual sense of the word about Hyndman. Whiles therefore, it might justly be considered a censurable affectation on the part of myself, and of those of like temperament with me, on public occasions to deck ourselves in a costume of this description, to Hyndman, who, as regards ways of living, distinctly has his conventional side, it was natural, and he might well have been accused of affectation (just as was Keir Hardie when he drove up to the House of Commons in 1892 in cycling knickerbockers and cloth cap) had he appeared otherwise. Anyway, those Bohemians who, like myself, are individualists in the matter of dress to the extent of claiming for themselves and conceding to every other man the social right to dress as he likes and as he deems suits him best, have no claim to cast stones at Hyndman for choosing to array himself in the conventional vesture of the privileged classes of his day and generation. While on the subject I may mention a couple of further illustrations of the conventionally "respectable" side of Hyndman's attitude in the matter of ways and manners. Hyndman is a great *raconteur*, and has always a store of amusing stories on hand. Now, most great *raconteurs* have a selection of *risqué* or smoking-room stories on their repertoires. With Hyndman this does not seem to be the case. Although I have often listened to stories of his, many of them very good ones, yet I have rarely if ever heard him relate anything calculated to bring the proverbial blush to the proverbial maidenly cheek. Not that Hyndman is by any means in general a votary of the Nonconformist conscience. He is, and claims to be, simply an ordinary man of the world. It is viewing him as such that I note this peculiarity as interesting.

Then, again, in the matter of drink. Hyndman is not an abstainer, or at least not on principle. On the contrary, he rather prides himself on his good taste in wines. Yet nevertheless he has often shown himself a rigid disciplinarian in the matter of temperance, especially as regards the proletarian. Always a man scrupulously moderate himself, he is inclined to be hard, many think excessively hard, not on drunkenness, which of course is out of the question, but on anything suggesting the idea of the very slightest excess in liquor in others, especially if those others happen to be working men. Of the above the following may be taken as an example. There had been a meeting somewhere in the Midlands one Sunday evening at which several members of the organization, including Hyndman, had taken part. They all returned to London in the same third-class saloon carriage on the Monday morning. Having some few hours' journey before them, some of the working-class members of the party bethought themselves to while away the time with a game of cards. No sooner had they taken their places alongside the narrow centre table than one of the "comrades" produced a bottle of whisky. Glasses and some water were procured, and the party proceeded to enjoy themselves. Our friend Hyndman, who was in another part of the carriage, passing along and observing the alcoholic debauch, could not restrain his indignation, and rebuked the men in well-set terms as acting in a disgraceful manner. Well, seeing there were some five or six persons among whom the bottle of whisky had to be divided in a three or four hours' journey, one would have thought that the potations per man could not be regarded in the light of a serious transgression. Hyndman, it would seem, thought otherwise. I was not present myself on the occasion, but have heard the story from two or three members of the party who strongly resented Hyndman's attitude. Of course, it must not be forgotten, as regards the story, that Hyndman has an original and quite peculiar aversion to the Keltic spirit above all other alcoholic beverages. So this may have had something to do with what to some may seem the extreme severity of his criticism on the conduct of the "comrades" on the occasion in question. Such are the minor merits or defects, according as we regard them, of our friend Hyndman's character. The importance of the role Hyndman has played as the protagonist of Socialism in England, and his influence generally on Labour politics, lends an interest even to small traits of character that in a lesser man would be unworthy of the attention of the recording angel. For the rest, Hyndman's career alike as a politician, an expositor of, and agitator for, Socialism, no less than as a journalist and writer on political and social questions in general, is an open book to the British public, and hence it is unnecessary to dilate upon it at greater length in these reminiscences.

One of the men who in the early days of the Social Democratic Federation was most active as a speaker and organizer was H.H. Champion, before referred to, the son of the late General Champion, and himself an ex-artillery officer. Champion had been out in India, and, I believe, resigned his commission in consequence of his disapproval of the Egyptian War of 1882, commonly known as the "Bondholders' War." This fact alone spoke for the man and rendered him sympathetic to Democrats and Radicals. On leaving the Army, Champion occupied a position in a publishing house, and before long bought an interest in a printing-office, where he continued to work as acting partner for some years. Champion had a short, incisive manner with him which undoubtedly impressed those with whom he came in contact. He was also an effective speaker, partly, doubtless, owing to the incisive manner spoken of, with many audiences. At first a devoted adherent of Hyndman, he seemed always possessed, as Hyndman himself put it, with an impatience to make twelve o'clock at eleven. This temperament of his caused him after a few years to tire of the slow and more or less monotonous business of agitating and organizing in the interests of Socialism, a kind of labour for which he possessed undoubted ability. Instead of continuing the work to which he had set his hand, after his first enthusiasm had spent itself, he developed a tendency for political intrigue with a view, as he in all probability sincerely thought, of obtaining immediate results in the improvement of the condition of the working classes and in general progress. The habit of intrigue once having laid hold of him, the tendencies which nearly always accompany it were not slow in showing themselves, and issued in acts towards former fellow-workers and friends of a nature which not only destroyed old ties of intimacy, but which no considerations of political expediency or anything else could, as most of us thought, morally justify. Owing perhaps to early family associations, Champion's intrigues were mainly connected with the Tory party, and conducted through acquaintances of doubtful political antecedents on the fringe of that party. In this way Champion became, from our point of view, politically completely demoralized, and the habit of political intrigue unfortunately, as already indicated, seemed not without a repercussion, for a time at least, on his general character and conduct. In himself Champion was by no means a bad sort. He had a certain

84

brightness and charm of manner combined with a ready mother-wit which made him good company in whatever society he found himself. I can well recall how, some years after the period here specially referred to, Champion was the life of a party of English delegates to the Zurich International Socialist Congress of 1893, one afternoon, in an excursion to Küssnacht, on the lake of Zurich. Notwithstanding that many of those present disliked and suspected him politically, all were more or less for the nonce under the spell of his personal magnetism. The Congress spoken of in Zurich, in the Summer of 1893, was, I believe, the last occasion, in Europe at least, when Champion figured at any Socialist function. Shortly after he emigrated to Australia, where he now lives in Melbourne. To me Champion was always friendly, and of his own accord sought to renew our acquaintance by correspondence a few years back; but the correspondence lapsed, owing, I imagine, to his dislike of my attitude in the matter of Female Suffrage and probably on the woman question generally. For Champion, since he has been in Australia, has apparently developed into a fanatical Feminist, owing perhaps, in part at least, to the family ties he has formed out there.

Another man also associated with the early days of the Socialist movement in England was James Leigh Joynes, who unfortunately died prematurely of heart-disease, now well-nigh a quarter of a century ago. Joynes was a master at Eton, as was his father before him. Of thoroughly Democratic sympathies, Joynes was practically compelled to resign his mastership owing to the action against him taken by the late Dr. Hornby, who was at that time head master of the college, in consequence of the publication of a little book by Joynes on the subject of a recent visit of his to Ireland – the Irish question being then uppermost – in which he strongly took the side of the tenants against the landlords and championed Home Rule and the Land League. As a matter of fact, the whole atmosphere of Eton was uncongenial to a man of Joynes's view's and temperament. The same remark, I believe, applies to Joynes's brother-in-law, Mr. H.S. Salt, the founder of the Humanitarian League, who also resigned from his Eton career at about the same time as Joynes. On leaving Eton, Joynes came up to live in London and devoted himself energetically for some time to political work as a member of the Federation. He did a good deal of free-lance journalism at this time, writing much for **Justice**, besides letters to the daily Press. He was the author, too, of many witty verses dealing with social questions, while his translations of the poems of Freiligrath, Herwegh, and others belonging to the period of the '48 movement in Germany, are admirably done. In January 1884 Joynes, in conjunction with myself, started the magazine **To-Day** as a monthly Socialist review. The list of contributors for the first six numbers embraces the names of Kegan Paul, Paul Lafargue, William Morris, William Archer, H.M. Hyndman, Boyd Kinnear, Edward Carpenter, Michael Davitt, E. Lynn Linton, "Stepniak," Havelock Ellis, etc. It may be interesting to note that the first publication of George Bernard Shaw's, viz. **The Unsocial Socialist**, was run as a serial through the first volume of **To-Day**. The story, the appearance of which in **To-Day** was the first introduction of Shaw to the public (if we except perhaps isolated letters to journals), excited considerable interest, and Hyndman declared that in Shaw lay the makings of an English Heine. How far time has confirmed this opinion may be left to the judgment of the reader. The review **To-Day** held its own throughout the year fairly well, but the "split" in the Socialist movement dealt with in the last chapter adversely affected it, and subsequently it passed into other hands, the late Hubert Bland ultimately becoming its editor. It appeared finally in a reduced form and at a lower price as the **International Review**, dying a natural death, I believe at the end of the eighties.

Joynes himself began to fail in health at the close of '81, and went in consequence, for change of air, to stop with some relations on his mother's side at Wiesbaden. He afterwards undertook a tour in Italy, returning to England in the Summer of 1885 apparently benefited. He spent some time with me at

Worthing, where I was at that time staying, soon after his return. On going back to London he conceived the idea of studying for the medical profession and entered himself at Middlesex Hospital. He continued his studies for a year or two, but the work was too much for him, and his health this time seriously broke down (he suffered from valvular disease of the heart), the result being that he had to abandon all idea of the medical profession and devote himself to invalidhood. Till now Joynes had been a strict vegetarian, but was induced by his medical adviser, perhaps under the circumstances with doubtful wisdom, henceforth to adopt a diet of butcher's meat. The change at least did him no good. Poor Joynes, it is true, lived on for a few years in Sussex, but as a confirmed invalid. He died on the 12th of February 1893 at East Grinstead, beloved and regretted by all who had known him.

John Burns, who had previously been active in the Secularist propaganda of Charles Bradlaugh, joined the SDF early in 1884. He is, as is well known, one of the best mass-meeting orators the country has produced. For the next three or four years from '84 onward Burns used his powers untiringly in the Socialist cause. Many of us can still remember the emphasis with which he insisted on Socialism, on a revolutionary reorganization of society, as the only hope for the working classes. He would have nothing of those who pretended that Teetotalism, Malthusianism, or even Trade-Unionism, would suffice to effect any essential improvement in the lot of the working class as a class. "I am a Trade-Unionist," he would say, "a practical Malthusian, a Teetotaller, and have always been so, and yet I remain for all these things what I was – a member of the working class, subsisting on a weekly wage." But as time went on, in spite of the part he played on the occasion of the disturbances of the 8th of February 1886 and the 21st of November 1887for his action on which latter occasion he suffered a month's imprisonment – towards the end of the eighties Burns slacked off in his revolutionary ardour. Like

Champion, he became afflicted with a desire to effect immediate results in practical politics, but, unlike Champion, he did not adopt a policy of intrigue with the fringe of the Tory camp. He made friends with certain Liberal and Radical politicians and proceeded to contest his native place, Battersea, as a Labour candidate, smiled upon by the Liberal party. His subsequent career is written in English political and labour history during the ensuing years.

Much severe criticism has been directed on Burns from the Socialist side, on account of his desertion of the SDF and of Socialist propaganda generally, for work on the lines of ordinary Liberalism. The criticism is doubtless well founded up to a point. Burns did in fact in practice, if not directly in theory, turn his back on the principles he had professed and the cause he had served for years past. It is only natural that his action should be resented by those who are convinced that the complete Socialist reorganization of society is the only thing seriously worth working for. On the other hand, I am unable to sympathize with the personal attacks, involving accusations of deliberate dishonesty, with which Burns has been assailed. For a Revolutionary Socialist by conviction it may be difficult to explain a change of front such as that of Burns otherwise than by the suggestion of personal motives of a questionable character. But let us look at the matter fairly. After four or five years of hard work at preaching the pure doctrine of Revolutionary Socialism, a man of Burns's energy of character sees little apparent result. He dwells on this aspect of things as it appears to him. Finally, the thought suggests itself, Would it not be better to let my revolutionary principles slide into the background for a while and throw in my lot with the ordinary Radical politicians by whose aid I may at least be able to effect some palliative reforms? This may be a commonplace attitude to take up, but it is undoubtedly one which appeals to a good many persons, and there is no ground, I contend, for assuming the man who adopts it, however much we may disagree with him, to be actuated necessarily by personally interested motives. Once in the swim of parliamentary life, we all know the *facilis descensus* effected by surroundings, including direct personal influences, to which most men are more or less amenable, in one way or another, without always themselves realizing that these influences are the real cause of modifications in their views and tendencies.

Burns, doubtless, has his faults, like other humans, but as far as my acquaintance with him goes, they seem to be mostly on the surface. He is often accused of having too good an opinion of himself. But after all, this probably refers to a certain, breezy self-confidence of manner not without *bonhomie* and hence not offensive. There is nothing "smug" about Burns, and "smug" conceit is after all the most intolerable form in which personal egotism manifests itself. As has been more than once remarked to me, Burns's entrance into the Cabinet made no difference in his manner. It never caused him "to put on side." As for mere material considerations, it must not be forgotten that Burns resigned his seat in the Cabinet with its £5,000 a year on a point of scrupulousness. There was nothing fundamental in his views either past or present which would not have justified him remaining in the Government, as Lloyd George and others did. He had never professed to be a Pacifist as some men count Pacifism. Neither did he find any extenuating circumstances for the Prusso-German Government in precipitating the war. He simply thought that a Labour member ought on principle to vote against appropriations for military purposes, and also that the country was unprepared for war on a great scale, as in fact it was. After all said and done, Burns, unlike some others, after he once turned to parliamentary life and current politics, never pretended to represent Socialism while acting the part of a *bourgeois* politician. He was at least honest in this way. The reader must not suppose from the foregoing that there is not much in Burns's political, and more especially administrative, action that I strongly disapprove. But there have been so many, as I consider, unfair attacks and insinuations respecting Burns's personal character on the part of Socialists, that I have felt bound to enter my humble protest on the other side.

Adolphe Smith, the expert on matters of sanitation, has already been alluded to in a forever chapter. From the time when he took part in the Paris Commune to the present day he has always been ready to give his services in any direction to help the Socialist movement.

Among the "old guard" of the SDF must not be forgotten the Viennese comrade, Andreas Scheu. An able and zealous open-air orator, Scheu was a personality who impressed himself upon all who came in contact with him chiefly through his vigorous utterance and the obvious sincerity of all he said. Whatever view he took up, he did so whole-heartedly, but he was a man withal of strong personal sympathies and antipathies. He was a great friend of William Morris, who liked his bluff and trenchant way of putting things as well as his inexhaustible enthusiasm.

A word must be said of the late Edward Aveling and Eleanor Marx Aveling, daughter of Karl Marx, with whom Aveling lived in relations of free marriage. The tragic end of Eleanor is well known. During the two last decades of her life she laboured unceasingly not only in the Socialist movement proper, but in the general working-class and Trade-Union movement. She it was who helped to found what is known as the New Unionism, being especially active in connexion with the Gasworkers and General Labourers' Union, at the meetings of which her speeches were often greeted by the men with the cry of "Good old stoker!" In appearance she was stout and took strongly after her father's side of the family, bearing a marked Jewish impress.

As for Edward Aveling, there is not much that is good to be said, save that he worked hard at times, although in a rather mechanical way, for Socialism, as he had before done for Secularism, when he was associated with the late Charles Bradlaugh. His reputation, financial, amatory, and otherwise, was very bad, but was kept afloat partly at least by the fact that stories ever and anon got into circulation about him which people believed on the ground of his general character, but which, as it happened, were not true, and when this was discovered it naturally had the effect of negatively improving his reputation by conveying the impression that if this story were false others might be so also, and that the man, after all, might be the victim of malicious tongues. As an illustration of this I will quote a story that went the round about Aveling at the time of the "split" in the SDF. It was to the effect that cheques were continually being drawn by William Morris in his favour. Now, it came out on the evidence of Morris himself that up to this time he had never given Aveling a single cheque or furnished him with money in any way. This was, of course, a great triumph for Aveling, who obtained credit and loans in various quarters in consequence. It is only fair to say that he also later made amends for his previous reticence in the matter of exigent borrowing in the case of Morris himself, All this shows the danger of crediting specific stories about a man on insufficient evidence, or merely on the strength of his general reputation, a habit that often has the effect of undeservedly buoying up a bad man's character. It is a habit, however, most people are very apt to acquire.

One of the early members of the SDF was Helen Taylor, stepdaughter of John Stuart Mill. Of a thin spare figure, her self-conceit was unbounded. She had a lofty smugness about her which had to be seen to be appreciated. Lecturing once at the Eleusis Club, she informed her audience that she would never marry, as she thought there was no man worthy of her. Elected a member of the School Board for London, she related one day at a meeting of the SDF council in my hearing that she had that morning been driving through the Borough to a meeting of the School Board, and had noticed groups of workmen sitting or standing (it was dinner-hour) at the side of the road, who looked up as she drove past and then turned to each other and nodded, as much as to say "There she is at her work!" The last phrase was delivered with a special *empressement* of the haw-haw tone which was habitual to her. The fact that the honest proletarians in question may not even have noticed her noble self, but merely indicated by their nods that they were agreeing that Challenger rather than Paladin was likely to win the chief race of that day, seems never to have entered the worthy lady's swelled head. And the funny part of it was that this preposterous creature, with her airs of pseudo-dignity, succeeded in imposing on otherwise sensible people, who at the council meetings of the SDF used to rise from their chairs as she majestically flaunted into the room. Morris did this at first, but on my remonstrating with him promised me not to do it any more. The good woman died, I believe, some years ago, in the bosom of the Catholic Church, attracted thither probably by the cult of the Virgin. The Christian Trinity of itself would have been doubtless much too masculine a proposition for her. Poor Mill!

A typical specimen of the London proletarian was J.E. Williams, an indefatigable as well as a popular agitator in the parks and at the street corners, in every way to which he could lay his hand in the cause of the working classes and of Socialism. He took part in public movements from his earliest years, and has remained true to his convictions from start to finish.

Another man of a different type who in his own way contributed his quota of work for the cause of Socialism at this time was Herbert Burrows. He was a member of the Democratic Federation from the beginning and did excellent propaganda service, especially in the Midlands, where his calling as a civil servant often took him. He is a well-known figure at Socialist congresses and Socialist funerals.

The proletarian leader of Socialism in this country with whom I was in closest personal touch was my old friend Harry Quelch. I have already given a sketch of his life and of my own relations with him, as an introduction to a volume consisting of a selection of his articles and short stories published shortly after his death by Messrs. Grant Richards & Co. Born at Hungerford, in Berkshire, in the late fifties, successively cattle-drover in his native place and, on coming to London as a young man worker in a tan-yard, and later on warehouseman packer to a firm in Cannon Street, then Trade Union secretary, and finally editor of **Justice**, Quelch was one of the most remarkable instances of the successfully self-educated man that I have ever met. He had a fine intellect, which readily grasped a subject in all its bearings, and was quick at assimilating new ideas when once placed before him. We used, whenever I was in London, to lunch together regularly once a week and discuss current events and the editorial policy of **Justice**. Quelch remained in harness almost to the last. When already struck by mortal illness, he accepted the invitation to deliver a course of lectures on Socialism at Ruskin College, Oxford, for which, at his request, I drew up a detailed syllabus that he seems to have closely followed. He died a few months after this, and was buried on September 20, 1913. His funeral was attended by a large concourse of Socialists of every shade, and speeches from the representatives of all the various Socialist organizations were made at the grave-side. Quelch is one of those men whom one never forgets. Always scrupulously loyal to his convictions, he was at once a clear thinker and an able and logical exponent of the views he professed.

No account of the history of Socialism in England would be complete without the mention of the indefatigable secretary for thirty years of the SDF, Henry William Lee. One cannot emphasize too much the debt that the old organization and the Socialist movement in England generally owes to the steady work of this energetic man. After the death of Quelch, Lee left the secretaryship of the old body to become the editor of the weekly paper **Justice**, where his abilities have proved equally effective in his new sphere of party usefulness.

Among the early pioneers of modern Socialism in Great Britain, George Bernard Shaw was conspicuous. At a later period successively journalist, critic in music, painting, and the drama, novelist, and last but not least, dramatic author, Shaw first became known to the British, and especially the London, public mainly as an eccentric; and unattached exponent and advocate of Socialist principles. He was zealous in attending meetings at this period and taking part in all discussions as they arose. There was scarcely an evening throughout the week when his voice and mother-wit were not to be heard in some hall or place of discussion in the metropolis or the suburbs, from the then existing Dialectical Society to the humblest workman's club where beer was drunk and pipes smoked. His Sundays were regularly booked for this latter class of resort. The audience was not infrequently poor alike in numbers and intelligence. He would even sometimes find clubs at which he had been invited to speak utterly unprepared to receive him. On one occasion he discovered the members of the club for which he was announced playing billiards, and arriving five minutes before the time fixed for the meeting, he inquired of the billiard players when and where the lecture he had been invited to give was to be held, receiving for reply the observation that they didn't "want no damn'd lecture," but intended going on with their game.

However, in spite of such small rebuffs as these, Shaw continued with praiseworthy diligence, and without receiving a penny of material reward, in his endeavours to instruct the London proletariat in the economics and politics of Socialism as he conceived it. At first, Shaw lectured often for the Social Democratic Federation and the Socialist League on general Marxist principles. Later on he attached himself to the group of Sidney Webb, Graham Wallas, Hubert Bland, and others, who founded the Fabian Society, the policy of which was opportunism and "permeation" of existing political parties and the intelligent middle classes generally with Socialist aims and policy, postponing direct propaganda for the realization of Socialism itself till a more convenient season. He and Sidney Webb concocted between them a new economic groundwork of Socialist theory based on Stanley Jevons's conception of "scarcity value" as being the measure of all value, which he designated by the name of "final utility."

Shaw at this time lived with his mother and sister in Fitzroy Street, N.W., and it was there that his earlier writings were produced, though some of them were not published until later. I may here relate an anecdote from this time illustrative of Shawesque humour. One evening Shaw and I had been to a meeting or a concert (I forget which), and on coming out we found it was a wet night. Shaw, although never at any time showing the usual symptoms of impecuniosity, happening at the moment to be short of pocket-cash, borrowed half-a-crown of me for a cab. The next day I duly received from G.B.S. a post-office order for the half-crown. Happening to meet Shaw again two or three evenings later with others, I mentioned the fact, and rallied him on his somewhat pedantic scrupulosity in taking the trouble to buy and forward a post-office order when he knew he would be seeing me again in a day or two and might have settled the matter then. "Oh!" said Shaw, "it is my habit to show punctilious accuracy in small money matters, so that when the time comes I may pull off my big coup with success. To achieve that it is absolutely essential to acquire a reputation for rigid and undeviating accuracy in small debts. The commonplace man does not understand that!"

The fame and fortune that have later come to Shaw through the brilliancy of his plays have doubtless to some extent spoiled him for general purposes. When a man has to live up to the character of being a perennial fountain of wit, the quality of the wit is often apt to become strained. As a matter of fact, if you analyse them you can reduce many of Shaw's effects to variations on one or two well-marked types. For instance, what I may teen the "paradox-joke" is a staple with Shaw. The following may be taken as a rough illustration of what I mean. The conversation turns on natural scenery, and especially mountain landscapes. On some one expatiating on these natural beauties, Shaw would, it is likely, at once start and maintain the thesis that Mont Blanc from the point of natural beauty is not a patch upon Primrose Hill. If you analyse it you will be astonished how much in Shawesque

95

humour is reducible to the type of this "paradox-joke." This he runs rather hard at times, as, for instance, when he asserts that he likes snobs. A paradox, of course, in itself often enshrines a profound truth which has been overlaid or distorted by the conventional thought of interested classes or of the multitude. It is the function of the paradox to unmask current pseudo-wisdom and to emphasize its real character. Now, it is the very importance of this true function of paradox in showing the hollowness of much in current opinion that passes for truth that renders it effective when used in the sense of a *reductio ad absurdum* – in other words, in the form of a joke. But the thing can be overdone, and when it is overdone it begins to pall. Once you detect the mechanism its effectiveness evaporates. It may fairly be questioned whether Shaw does not run at least very near the limit of the legitimate employment of the "paradox-joke," if it is to be an efficient instrument of wit and wisdom.

But apart from this side-issue, as many will regard it, the question arises, Is Shaw's work as literature likely to survive in the sense of becoming an English classic? This is a difficult question to answer with anything like decision. Yet I think there is some ground for believing that some at least of it will. Shaw's points, though many of them are topical and hence are destined increasingly to lose their force, have nevertheless a present freshness in them which will give them a good start, and probably run them through at least a couple of generations with their smartness but slightly dulled. This was the case with Dickens, who is only now beginning to show sere and yellow to the appreciation of the younger contemporary generation. Such, of course, is the inevitable fate of all literature dealing essentially with contemporary manners and customs or with contemporary issues. But the warding off of the time when "points" begin to be blunted and interests dulled is itself an evidence of genius of no mean order. The further problem then is, Will the work, having lost its special kind of interest when written, renew its youth like the eagle's, in acquiring the riper and more dignified position of a classic? Will mankind ever place Shaw in the rank of Dickens, Thackeray, Heine, Balzac, etc.? Time will show. Meanwhile the question remains an interesting subject of speculation for the literary-minded.

I come now to talk of the man who, after H.M. Hyndman, occupied the most prominent place in the public eye as a pioneer of Modern Socialism in Great Britain, though the prominence attached to the name of William Morris in this connexion was originally largely due to his already acquired fame as a poet and authority on decorative art. I first met Morris in the early Spring of 1883, and later at the annual conference of the then Democratic Federation, which he had recently joined. As stated on a former page, I induced him to allow himself to be nominated for the Executive Council after he had first declined. In view of later developments, and of the way in which the Socialist movement absorbed his time and energies during the ensuing years, Morris often used to chaff me with what I had let him in for, remarking of himself, "he little thought when he set out of running such a rig." In his connexion with Socialism the typical vehemence of energy and enthusiasm of Morris's nature were conspicuously exhibited. Whatever he took up with, he threw himself into it heart and soul. For four or five years after he had definitively joined that movement, Socialism both in its theory and as a practical propaganda occupied the first place in his thoughts. All his other work fell for the time into the background. To relate all the incidents of my close association with Morris during the years in question would occupy too much space in these reminiscences, but a few illustrative of Morris's character may be given.

If there was one trait especially characteristic of Morris's disposition it was his good-heartedness and genial jollity. He liked good cheer for himself and others. The thing he hated most as a view of life was Puritanism in all its aspects. While in no way countenancing intemperance, or for that matter serious excess of any kind, he abominated teetotalism as he did every

97

other form of ascetic fanaticism. He was a thorough Pagan in the best sense of the word, who believed in living and letting live. With the mortification of the flesh in any form he had no sympathy. Such being Morris's general attitude to life in its everyday aspects, it will surprise no one to hear that he would never meet a friend without "standing drinks." He was indeed generous to a fault in every way. Being regarded as a good quarry by impecunious anarchist refugees from the East of Europe, he would keep a drawer full of half-crowns for almsgiving in this kind. They called in, he told me, and began to narrate stories in unintelligible English, which he generally cut short by the production of one or more of these half-crowns, according as the personality of the visitor seemed sympathetic or not, and this generally had the effect of causing him to leave with thanks. Morris kept open table at which visitors used to call in casually to take "pot-luck." He was strongly averse to all formality, and neither gave dinner-parties in the ordinary sense nor attended them if he could help it. But he was always glad to see his friends drop in at any meal. Evening dress he never wore, or a frock-coat. In fact, it is impossible to picture Morris otherwise than in his well-known garb, consisting of a dark blue serge suit and blue shirt without cravat and a "wide-awake" hat. Morris was a Bohemian through and through. But good-natured and warm-hearted though he was, Morris could at times become a prey to the most violent fits of passion, in which he objurgated freely. As a rule, however, these fits, probably attributable to gout (uric acid in the system), only lasted for a few minutes, after which hiss habitual *bonhomie* reasserted its sway. In fact, if anything, he seemed to think it incumbent on himself to be more than usually amiable to the objurgated person after one of the fits in question.

Morris's solicitude for his friends' safety and welfare was always a noticeable trait in his character. On one occasion I had the intention of going to Sicily especially to visit the ruins of Agrigentum (Girgenti). Now at the time there had been some talk of brigandage in Sicily. Morris, on my mentioning my idea to him, insisted upon my not deciding to go before consulting his friend Richmond, the painter, who knew Sicily well. Accordingly, we repaired forthwith to Mr. Richmond's house in Hammersmith. We found the distinguished artist suffering from gout and sitting up in bed reading Jowett's **Plato**. The upshot was that, although the danger did not seem very great, Morris thought, all things considered, I had better abandon the idea of Sicily for the time being. "There is another point, Bax," he said; "if anything should happen it might mean my having to stump up a thousand pounds or so cash at a moment's notice, which, though of course I should do it if necessary, would still be inconvenient to me just at the present time." I should mention that some such sum had shortly before been paid as ransom for an Englishman captured by brigands. Needless to say, after this expression of Morris's view the projected expedition was abandoned.

Another less pleasant incident illustrating the same forethought I may here give. Once, during a few days' walking tour in Sussex, somewhere between Pulborough and Midhurst, we were passing through some fields by the side of a stream. Suddenly Morris became morose and unsociable in manner. A little while after again coming upon the highroad we turned into an inn for luncheon. Sitting after the meal, I asked Morris the reason of his grumpiness. He replied that he was much exercised in passing through those fields in that he saw bulls regarding us in a more or less menacing manner, and that although he himself could have escaped by swimming across the little river, knowing that I could not swim, he was perplexed as to what course to pursue in the event of a bovine attack. Hence his surliness.

Morris was all his life an indefatigable historical student. His knowledge of the by-ways of history was marvellous. To this he added, especially latterly, the study of comparative mythology and what may be termed the newer anthropology. His love for the Middle Ages as well as for early society generally, but especially as exemplified in early Gothic and Germanic life, is notorious, and is notably enshrined in some of his later prose works.

However, I discussed with him once what historical surroundings one would wish to be reborn into after the manner suggested in Plato's myth of Er, and on the question being raised whether it would be preferable to be reincarnated as a mediaeval baron of the twelfth century or an Athenian Eupatrid of the fifth century B.C., to my surprise he seemed inclined to "opt" for the "Athenian gentleman," on the ground of the general intellectual life of the classic epoch, as against the rudeness of existence in the medieval castle. The choice would be an obvious one to the average cultivated man, but for Morris, with his love of the Gothic, the barbaric, and the medieval, it came to me somewhat as a surprise. For my own part I should always choose to be reborn into a country retreat somewhere on the shores of the Eastern Mediterranean in the second century under the Antonines. Friedrich Engels once observed to me that so far as he was concerned he should give his vote for a new lease of life to the Italian Renaissance of the fifteenth century.

The falling off in Morris's vigour during the last year or two of his life was painful to witness. As the kidney disease from which he suffered advanced, in spite of occasional flashes of his old energy, his powers were obviously ebbing away. He died on the 21st of September 1896. A cruise he had taken a few weeks before in Norwegian waters for the benefit of his health not only failed in its object, but – which shows the complete decay of his powers, mental and physical – did not seem to excite any special interest in him.

Morris's views on literature were decided and peculiar. Among English poets he did not care for Wordsworth, while his admiration for Byron and Shelley was moderate. Of Coleridge he had a very high opinion. Among the moderns, Tennyson he liked, but Browning failed altogether to appeal to him as a poet. He thought him a vain man personally. He used to say that when he met him in society Browning always pretended to have forgotten who he was. For the smaller fry he did not care much. Among novelists, Dickens held an especially high place with him. He was, it should be said, an omnivorous novel-reader. Of the old painters Giotto was his great hero, and among contemporaries his old friend with whom he used to breakfast religiously every Sunday morning, Burne-Jones. To William Morris, when one thinks of him, the somewhat hackneyed quotation from *Hamlet* seems notably to apply – "He was a man, take him for all in all," we "shall not look upon his like again." For Morris was a specially striking personality. As a friend of his expressed it to me, "by his death one felt as though a piece of one's own life had been cut out."

In the present chapter I have gathered together impressions of the most prominent leaders of the Socialist movement at the time of its inception in this country. They all, with the exception of Shaw, originally belonged to the Social Democratic Federation. Of course, names will be missed of men who have subsequently become identified with one or another form of Socialism in Great Britain. The Independent Labour Party and the Fabian Society have both produced many such. To have included them in this place would have carried us too far. Of many, their Socialism is open to criticism, to say the least, and although the present writer has had no personal quarrels with any of them, their introduction into the present chapter would have necessarily suggested polemical discussions which lie outside its scope and purpose.

An exception may be made, however, in the case of one figure, namely that of Ben Tillett. Ben first came into prominence through the part he played in the Great Dock Strike of 1889. The account of the strike and its inner working he has himself given in an ably written pamphlet. Ever since this great landmark in the history of English labour, Ben Tillett, the secretary of the Transport Workers' Union, has been to the fore in all labour disputes. At first, while recognizing his ability as an agitator and an organizer, I was not altogether impressed with his attitude, in which I thought I detected signs of a certain philandering with the Nonconformist conscience and the section of the *bourgeoisie* connected therewith. Whether this were so or not at that time may be doubtful, but in any case the fault, if it ever existed, was short-lived with Tillett, who has since come out as a thoroughgoing Socialist and a member of the Socialist movement. I first became personally acquainted with Tillett in 1903, on the occasion of a meeting of the Labour party of Southampton to choose their parliamentary candidate for the next election. The two men in the field were he and my old friend Harry Quelch. I may confess that before going to the meeting both Quelch and I regarded the nomination of Tillett as a hostile move and Tillet himself as a dangerous adversary. What was our surprise when, on joining Ben before the meeting, we found that though he had accepted the nomination in form and had come down to Southampton ostensibly as a counter-candidate to Quelch, he had done so with the intention of throwing the whole weight of his support into the scale for Quelch In a brilliant speech Tillett proclaimed his Socialism and urged his hearers to vote for Quelch as the best man they could have to represent them. The chivalrous and unselfish conduct on this occasion of Ben, who up to this time had not been regarded as a declared Socialist, naturally endeared him throughout the ranks of the SDF.

As a *raconteur* Ben is in his way inimitable. I shall never forget his description of the trial of a Chinaman in Australia, brought up before a police-court for a petty theft; the lengthy colloquy of the prisoner and his interpreter being given in due style, with reminiscences of the Chinese language, which on the final demand of the weary magistrate as to what the prisoner really had to say for himself, resulted in the interpreter's laconic reply, "Please, your Honour, he says he didn't do it!" The duologue with its anti-climax was given as only Ben can give it.

There is probably no one in England who has the same power of holding and managing the most unruly or the roughest crowd with the magic of his words as Ben Tillett. In a strike he is the one man most hated and most feared by the capitalist class. The popular idea is that Ben Tillett is the typical fomenter of strikes. Nothing can be more untrue. For instance, in the Transport Workers' strike of 1912 Tillett, as secretary of the Union, strongly opposed the strike. It was only when once decided upon by the Union against his own wishes that he threw himself, as in duty bound, heart and soul into it, in order to make the best of things. As a matter of fact, no labour leader wants a strike for its own sake. He has everything to lose and nothing to gain by it. If it fails or anything goes wrong, all the blame of the men falls upon his shoulders. If it is successful – "Well! He's only done his duty." (*Voilà tout.*) The hatred and abuse of the employing class and their Press he receives in full measure in either case. This notion of the labour leader being a strike promoter is one of the most foolish of the many foolish ideas entertained by the middle classes on labour matters. But, as Trinculo says in the *Tempest*, "adversity makes us acquainted with strange bedfellows," and one is strongly reminded of this when one reads of the obnoxious strike-promoting Ben being smiled upon, and his recruiting meetings presided over, by dukes and other pillars of the State, as has been the case during the great European War.

# VI. Personalities of the Socialist Movement on the Continent

The modern Socialist movement on the continent of Europe preceded the movement in England by some decades. The imaginative faculty of the continental workman is, as a rule, much stronger than that of his English colleague, and without an appreciable amount of what we may term constructive imagination in the masses, no world-historic movement can get under way. Then in all the principal continental countries there has been a revolutionary tradition that is wanting in Great Britain. Even the Chartist movement of the thirties and forties was a flash in the pan, so far as revolutionary action was concerned, and hence could supply no starting-point for a revolutionary tradition such as we meet with in so many continental countries. More than this, its failure before the advancing tide of Liberalism rather tended to damp down, or we might even say to kill off, all ideas of drastic revolutionary change. This may at least partly account for the obtuseness of the British working classes even to grasp, still more to become enthusiastic for, an ideal outside the range of current politics, or, indeed, to concern themselves with aught beyond the sordid issues of the moment, such as a trifling rise in the rate of wages, etc. This is partly due to lack of education and knowledge of history, which leads the British workman to the view that things as they are and were in his lifetime were always so and ever shall be, and that any idea of a fundamental change in social and economic relations is unworthy of the attention of the sensible, practical man that he is. In most continental countries, on the other hand, the workman is better educated than here, and owing to this and his greater imaginative grasp of things, is able to look forward to the future in a manner alien to the average uneducated English mind, more especially as that mind was constituted during the middle and even later decades of the nineteenth century Hence the priority and the more effective spread of Socialist ideas in the minds of the continental working class that have hitherto been so noticeable.

Of all European countries, the revolutionary tradition is, and has been since the Great Revolution, strongest in France. Hence France throughout the middle period of the nineteenth century was regarded as *par excellence* the home of political and social revolution. At the same time the great '48 movement seized Europe from end to end, and so created a democratic revolutionary tradition in countries such as Germany (for instance), where, in spite of the prince-made wars which had devastated it, such a tradition had before been almost wholly absent. If the first suggestions of Modern Socialism in theory are to be found in the Communist manifesto, in practical political life the first attempts, vague and inchoate though they may have been, are to be looked for in the French Red Republican movement of '48. Between this period and the Paris Commune of 1871 the first International was founded, and about the same time, or, a little before, arose the first beginnings of German Social Democracy. The International took root and spread in France, especially in Paris. The ideas of the old French Red Republican party began to grow in clearness, although it was still nebulous as regards many of its elements. Then came that epoch-making event for modern Socialism, the Paris Commune. I have already briefly dealt with the Paris Commune, and I need only here remind the reader that the Commune was the first government manned by the working classes and which had the Socialistic reorganization of society as its aim. The Paris Commune, therefore, and the year 1871 afford us a convenient date for reckoning the birth of the modern Socialist movement in the wider form in which we have known it during the last decades of the nineteenth and the opening years of the present century. The beginnings, of course, in various lands date from an earlier period, as already pointed out; but from the seventies onward the Socialist movement in all countries has become a world-movement, the importance of which is universally recognized, which cannot be said of the earlier and more local movements out of which it developed.

As already explained in an earlier chapter, the Commune it was that awakened me, as it awakened many others, to an interest in the Social problem, and the first Socialists that I met were members or adherents of the Commune. There was Pascal Grousset, a handsome man, who in the later seventies was a regular attendant at the British Museum Reading-room. About the time referred to, I used to see a good deal of him, and often talked over the Commune. He deplored the want of initiative and of a coherent policy which characterized it. He also told me how ignorant the non-political Parisians were of the actual facts of the struggle going on around them. During the *semaine sanglante,* he said – at a time, that is, when the unfortunate Communards were being butchered by the Versailles troops on all sides – he overheard a woman saying to a child she had in her arms, in tones of indignation, "*Oui, oui, mon petit, nous nous rappelerons de la Commune, nous, n'est-ce pas?*" the idea being, of course, that the communards were the slaughterers, instead of the slaughtered.

During their exile in London, the adherents of the Commune used to celebrate the outbreak of the insurrection of the 18th of March by a banquet in a French hotel named, if I remember rightly, the "Hotel de la Cloche," in one of the passages off Holborn. I was present by invitation on one of these occasions (1880), when I remember that Charles Longuet, who married Jenny Marx, Karl Marx's eldest daughter, and became father of Jean Longuet, at present editor of **l'Humanité** and member of the Chamber, made a speech in which he set forth the failure of the Commune to achieve its ends as being due to the fact that the Commune had to struggle with the military situation throughout. This hampered its social and economic work, while at the same time it was unable to cope with the military situation itself. Hartmann, the Russian Nihilist, was present at this anniversary dinner. Dr. Albert Regnard, the secretary of police under the Commune, a man with an extraordinarily impressive head and, like Pascal Grousset, a constant student at the British Museum, was also present. Charles Longuet, Paschal Grousset, and Albert Regnard are all three long since dead, as also Camélinat, the governor of the Tuileries during the Commune, and many others who were there. Of those who took a leading part in the events of the Spring of '71 there are few, if any, survivors left. The last time I met some of the "old guard" together was about the January of 1899, at a little friendly gathering one evening in a cafe somewhere off the Boulevard St. Michel. "Papa" Longuet, as he was called, I saw, however, for the last time at a luncheon party at his house in the Autumn of 1900, after the Paris Congress of that year.

Of the newer men of the French Socialist movement, the one who played the most prominent role was Jean Jaurès. He came noticeably to the front in the later years of the nineties. Jaurès studied for an academic career at the University of Paris, and was a contemporary of the celebrated Henri Bergson as a student. Subsequently he became Professor of Philosophy at the University of Toulouse. His strikingly brilliant oratorical powers are known to all the world. Staunch and consistent to his declared convictions throughout his whole political career, his fairness and rigid impartiality of judgment procured him the esteem of men of all parties. His achievements in the way of work were something extraordinary. With all his parliamentary duties he found time to write a detailed and carefully documented history of the French Revolution, perhaps the best existing. As a conversationalist, Jaurès was not so striking as he was as an orator. A nervous twitching of the eyes, especially when in Company, vas a marked characteristic. Jaurès nevertheless had remarkably persuasive powers in dealing with men. No other man could have succeeded in uniting the apparently irreconcilable sections of the French Socialist party and welding them into an organized whole as Jaurès did after the Amsterdam Congress of 1904. This was the more remarkable a triumph of personal magnetism and of the respect inspired by character, seeing that Jaurès had undoubtedly played a distinctly opportunist role during the Combos administration. His bowing to the decision of the Amsterdam Congress, which was practically a condemnation of his attitude in the matter in question, was an act of self-abnegation which showed a true sense of Internationalism. Altogether, Jean Jaurès was a rare personality. Possessed of personal amiability combined with extraordinary powers alike in the intellectual and practical spheres, and an integrity of character not merely moral, but political as well, which was absolutely stainless, it is difficult to find his equal as an all-round man, at once a capable theorist and a remarkable leader.

Another very different personality, well known in French Socialist circles at one time, although as a political force somewhat of an *homme manqué*, was Paul Lafargue, who married Laura, the second daughter of Karl Marx. A pleasant and genial fellow, who had sat at the feet of Marx himself and was an intimate friend of Engels, Lafargue was chiefly known as a writer of propagandist pamphlets, of which the most popular was the **Droit a la Paresse**, and polemical essays on the materialist theory of history, on Marxian lines. He was, however, elected to the Chamber once, though he failed to make his mark there. His writings were vivacious and clear, but for the most part superficial and without originality. He was a striking-looking man personally, with a dash of negro blood in his veins. His devotion to his wife was extraordinary, and they committed suicide together by means of morphia injection early in 1912 in his house at Draveil, near Paris, the alleged ground being dread of approaching old age, though some say financial embarrassment was the cause. He was close upon seventy and his wife a few years younger. Lafargue, as I knew him, was a fairly well-to-do man, but had the reputation, whether justly or unjustly, of being somewhat close in money matters, for which reason, I suppose, he obtained the nickname in the French party of le *petit épicier*.

An abler man than Lafargue and, like Jaurès, a powerful

orator, is Jules Guesde, who became a member of the first French coalition War Ministry. An intimate personal friend of Lafargue, he was the leader of the specially orthodox Marxian wing of the French Socialist movement. Tall and striking, with his long black beard, Guesde has been an impressive figure at all International Socialist Congresses. His uncompromising zeal for the purity of the party in the sense of its rigid adhesion to principle, and his abhorrence of all contamination with the trickery of *bourgeois* party politics, were notable features of his policy and speeches on all such occasions. I shall never forget the fiery and powerful attack he made at the Amsterdam Congress of 1904 on the policy of Jaurès at that time, which favoured the participation (under suitable guarantees, of course) of Socialists in the work of existing governments. Jaurès, as already stated, subsequently receded from this position in deference to the decision of the International Congress, and was instrumental in the formation of the French United Socialist party, on which, of course, Guesde and Jaurès became reconciled. Guesde has been accused recently of dereliction of principle in having joined the coalition French Ministry. It may fairly be argued, however, that the principle of abstention from co-operation with non-Socialists or anti-Socialist governments, even in matters where they are prepared to make concessions from a Socialist point of view, does not apply to the abnormal conditions arising from a national crisis precipitated by an invasion and the presence of a hostile foreign force on the national territory. Besides, the case of a coalition government in normal times is quite different. In an ordinary government the theory is that complete unity and solidarity obtain as between its members. The mere participation, therefore, in such a government necessarily indicates, at the very least, bare assent to all its measures, and to give even this implied assent to measures, many, or probably most, of which will be designed with the purpose of bolstering up the present capitalist system in some form or shape, is obviously inconsistent for a Socialist who is the sworn enemy of that system. The case of a coalition ministry in time of War, however, is by no means the same. Here there is no pretence of agreement on any other point than the desire to provide the most effective organization for the national defence, and there is no question of any legislation not bearing on this one question being introduced. Hence, whether advisable or unadvisable as a matter of expediency in a particular case, I fail to see any breach of essential consistency in the course adopted by Jules Guesde as regards France, or for that matter by Emile Vandervelde as regards Belgium, in joining the coalition Ministries of their respective countries. The divergencies of view and hostility between various members of such coalition ministries are openly and directly admitted on any or on all points lying outside the immediate purpose for which the government in question has been formed. This being so, membership of an emergency cabinet of this sort does not, I contend, necessarily infringe the principle of abstention from co-operation with non-Socialist political parties.

Other of the later leaders of Socialism in France I have met on different occasions, but have not known more closely. If I remember rightly, I sat with Aristide Briand at the London Congress at Queen's Hall in 1896 on the Standing Orders Committee. The late Charles Vaillant, the old member of the Commune, was also there.

Turning from France to its eastern neighbour, little Switzerland, in taking note of the proletarian and Socialist movement, one can hardly fail to remark as one of its foremost representatives the name and figure of Hermann Greulich, the Labour Secretary for the Swiss Confederation. The shaggy figure of Greulich, with its shock head of white hair and ragged beard and its rough garb, of which the homespun jersey generally forms a part, has been prominent at all Socialist Congresses. Greulich is an autodidact, and a very remarkable one. Born in Breslau in 1843, of poor parents, he was apprenticed to the bookbinding trade, after having received the ordinary school education. During the *Lehrjahre* and *Wanderjahre*, which at that time formed part of the curriculum through which every skilled workman in Germany had to pass, Greulich improved every occasion for self-education. This he has continued throughout his life. As a young man Greulich emigrated to Switzerland, becoming a Swiss citizen, and ultimately settling in Zürich. What is remarkable in Greulich is his all-round culture. He is not merely well read in the literature of Socialism, in general economics, or in the aspects of industrial history, having an especial bearing on the present conditions of the working class, but there are few departments in which he is not equally grounded. Greulich has all the qualifications of a scholar and what the Germans call a *Schöngeist*, and would have doubtless made a name for himself in scholarship or in literature had he been born in different circumstances. As it is, his conversation never fails to leave the impression of a man of wide reading and independent thought.

As might be expected, no name throughout the working-class and Socialist movement of Switzerland is better known than that of Hermann Greulich. It is a curious circumstance that Greulich has been the victim more than once of false reports of his death. Some years ago one of my sons, returning from a visit to New York, told me that a report was current in Swiss circles there that Greulich was dead. I immediately wrote to him stating that I had heard he was dead, but hoped it was not true. A few days later I received a reply from him that he was not dead, although he had not been very well lately.

Singularly enough, not very long after this another report of his death arose, and this time in Zürich itself. The rumour spread very widely that the well-known labour leader, parliamentary representative, cantonal and municipal counsellor, Hermann Greulich, was no more. That evening the Choral Society of Zürich, of which Greulich was an active and influential member, met for rehearsal, when the conductor, on taking his seat at the desk, addressed the society on the sad news of the loss they had sustained in the death of one who had done so much for the society and for choral music in Switzerland generally. He invited his hearers to rise in their places as a sign of

112

respect for the deceased before proceeding with the work of the evening. This act of homage was only just performed when Greulich himself walked in. Already in the afternoon of the day the same rumour had spread round the shores of the lake, where silk-weaving factories and other industrial establishments are situated. In many of these the workmen demanded that work should cease for the day as befitting the occasion of the loss of the great Swiss labour leader. This was objected to by the employers, and after some altercation the matter was arranged by the compromise that work should continue that day till the usual hour, but that the factory should be closed altogether on the day of the funeral. Accordingly, the same evening a committee was formed for celebrating the obsequies, wreaths bought, and a speaker chosen to deliver the funeral oration. Next day that committee dissolved.

I remember very well one afternoon sitting with Greulich in the Labour Bureau, when the late Sir Randall Cremer, whom I knew slightly, appeared seeking some piece of information or other. I had to act as interpreter for Sir Randall, who did not speak German. The upshot was an invitation for Greulich and myself to dine with him that evening at the Bellevue Hotel, where he was staying, to meet the late Sir John Lubbock (afterwards Lord Avebury), who was also a guest there. We went and met sir John, but I am bound to say the distinguished man did not impress Greulich or myself as giving evidence of any great intellectual power in his manner and conversation. whether the report was true that his books were by no means entirely original, but largely the work of "ghosts," I am unable to say. On the other hand, it is of course undeniable that the capacities of able men by no means always translate themselves into an impressive personality in social intercourse.

The German Social Democratic party, owing to various circumstances, to its direct connexion with the chief founder of modern scientific Socialism, to its rapid growth and consequent numerical greatness, as well as to its perfect organization, acquired up to the outbreak of the war in 1914 a certain hegemony over the International Socialist movement as represented by the National Socialist parties of other countries. Hence the German party, as it existed from its inception until recent years, has a unique interest and importance of its own. Latterly, of course, as many of us had long suspected, and as events have proved, it had degenerated into a favourable nest for political intriguers and adventurers of the worst type. But this is a development of the last twenty years, and, indeed, in its worst form, of much less time. It was not always so. And even now there is no evidence at present forthcoming that the defection and corruption of the majority of its actual parliamentary leaders is shared in by the bulk of the rank and file. There can be no doubt, however, that impatience with mere propaganda, and the desire to play a rôle in current, or as it would be termed "practical," politics, has prepared for mans- years past a suitable soil for "Revisionists" and political tricksters of all sorts. On the other hand, in the conduct of the party from its early beginnings in the sixties to near the end of the nineties of the last century there is no serious breach of principle that can be charged against it as a whole. For the earlier period I refer, of course, to the Marxian party. The followers of Lassalle were always Nationalist. The question of Internationalism was indeed one of the great bones of contention between them and the Marxians. The tendency of the Lassallian party, moreover, was undoubtedly not without inclinations to traffic with non-Socialist parties. But from the union of the two sections at Erfurt in 1875, when the bulk of the Lassallian section accepted the Marxian programme in its entirety, until, let us say 1895, although mistakes may have been made by individual members, there was nothing in the conduct of the party as a whole calculated to forfeit the respect and confidence of the Socialists of other countries.

Now, the personalities with whom I was best acquainted in the German movement were those who flourished in the period named – the so-called "old guard" of German Social Democracy.

114

The names of the late Wilhelm Liebknecht, of the noble conduct of whose heroic son Karl we have heard so much during the present war, August Bebel, Paul Singer, and others less known to the outside public, will hold a distinguished and an honourable place in the history of the Socialist movement for all time. My introduction to the men of the German movement during the eighties was in the main, directly or indirectly, through Friedrich Engels. Karl Kautzky, upon whom the mantle of Engels as theorist of the German movement fell after the latter's death, I met first at Engel's house in Regent's Park Road. Bernstein I first saw in Zürich in 1886. He was then editing the party organ, the **Sozialdemokrat**, there, it being during the period when Bismarck's anti-Socialist legislation was in force. Of several of the then prominent members of the party I made the personal acquaintance at Zürich and St. Gallen, at the time of the great party Congress held at the latter town in October 1887. This Congress was necessarily, under the, circumstances, of a more or less secret character. I was invited to attend by the executive council of the party, the members of which arrived in Zürich from Germany a few days before the Congress met. Our train was received at the St. Gallen station by a committee of trusty party men, who had been in the town already for a day or two, organizing the arrangements, and who conducted us to the inn "Zum Schönen Weg," some two miles out. I remember that Grillenberg, the Reichstag member for Nürnberg, who had come by a previous train, and had been followed from Germany by a Government spy, on remonstrating at being dogged by this man, was assaulted by him with a life-preserver and left bleeding on the road. He was, however, taken to the house of a friendly inn keeper in St. Gallen for recovery. The proceedings of the Congress lasted nearly a week, and during this time I naturally came into close relations with all the more important members of the movement, lodging in the same *Gasthaus* with Liebknecht, Bebel, Singer, Auer, Hasenclever, etc. Not one of these men of the "old guard" of the German party is now living. Among the burning issues discussed at this Congress was a vote of censure

115

on certain members of the party for having supported a Goverment project, to wit, the construction of the so-called Baltic Canal. The majority of the party, including all the leaders with the exception, I think, of Hasenclever, were for maintaining in its integrity the principle of opposition to all important Government enterprises. This Congress of the German party of October 1888 created considerable sensation at the time, as it was the first that had been held since the passing of the anti-Socialist law.

Old Wilhelm Liebknecht, who died in 1900, I often met during the ensuing years both at Socialist congresses and in private. But the man with whom I came most in contact among the leaders of the "old guard" of German Social Democracy was August Bebel. This was largely owing to the fact that Bebel, whose daughter Frieda married and was living in Zürich, built himself a house at Küssnacht, about three miles from the town, on the lake. Many are the discussions on points of Socialist policy, on the woman question, etc., I have had with him during these years. I can recall one incident of a somewhat amusing character to those who witnessed it. One evening I had crossed the lake to Küssnacht from a place on the other side with some friends. At Küssnacht we boarded the steamer going to Zürich. Bebel was on deck with a group of companions. Among my own party was a Socialist from Köln, who had fled to Switzerland, having been threatened with a prosecution for some article he had written in the local party organ. Now, it should be said that a ukase had recently been issued by the Council of the part that those threatened with prosecutions of this kind should not flee, but "face the music." The immediate occasion of this decision was the fact that certain persons, having expatriated themselves for the foregoing, reason and not finding employment whither they had gone, had become a financial charge upon the party. Such, however, was not the case with the person in question, who had sufficient means of his own to live on. Hence he maintained that the rule referred to did not in intention apply to his case. Bebel, however, took the view of the stern moralist, fearing, as he afterwards told me, that the comrade in question would tend to become demoralized by the idle life he was leading, being still quite a young man. Accordingly, with perhaps questionable tact, Bebel seized the occasion of meeting the unfortunate Rhinelander on the steamer for rebuking him severely for his conduct in not only infringing party discipline, but withdrawing himself from his legitimate sphere of usefulness. The scene was distinctly humorous. There stood on the deck of the steamer our passive Rhinelander, looking rattier "small," while his party leader, confronting him, poured forth a flood of admonishing rebukes, the two principal actors in the scene being surrounded by an audience of some twenty persons, consisting of friends, acquaintances, and casual outsiders.

I chaffed Bebel afterwards at the exhibition of the Rhinelander in the rôle of the poor sinner being rebuked by his father-in-God. Bebel pleaded that he had only acted with the best intentions for the man's good. The man himself, however, apparently took this matter otherwise, and a few days later, at a little dinner-party given by a mutual friend to which our Rhinelander, Bebel, and myself were invited, the Rhinelander was conspicuous by his absence.

My intercourse with the circle in Zürich in which Bebel moved belonged mainly to the nineties of the last century. It was not confined to members of the Socialist party, but included some men of the '48 period, already, as may be imagined, having attained "the sere and yellow" stage. Most of them were refugees from Germany who had settled down in Switzerland on the collapse of the '48 revolutionary movement. The somewhat belated ideas of these good men and their want of understanding of modern Socialism were amusing and instructive.

The later years of Bebel's political career were somewhat clouded for many of his Socialist comrades by the unfortunate speech suggestive of jingoism which he made in the Reichstag in March 1907. Returning from the South of France through Zürich a few weeks after its delivery, I there met his wife, Julia Bebel.

117

On my expressing my regrets at the pronouncement in question, she entirely agreed, remarking, "I told August that he had made a great mistake and that his statements would be resented by many." This was the last time I saw her, for she died a few months later. Bebel himself lived six years longer, being found dead in his bed on the 20th August 1913, at a health resort near Chur, in Eastern Switzerland.

Talking of the German party and its "old guard," I must not forget my old friend the "Red Postmaster," as he was called, from the fact of his having organized the transmission to Germany from Zürich of the **Sozialdemokrat** during the period of the anti-Socialist law. Julius Motteler had been a member of the Reichstag from the beginning. A Swabian by birth, he early became attached to the party, where his exceptional abilities as an organizer soon made him one of its most indispensable members. His steady and unswerving devotion throughout his life to his ideals (he died in 1907, aged seventy) and his amiability of character have left an ineffaceable memory with those who knew him.

Of the leaders of the Austrian party, though I have met them all at congresses and elsewhere, the one with whom I have had most personal intercourse is the original founder of the party, and still its leading representative, Victor Adler. Adler devoted a considerable part of his personal fortune to organizing the Austrian movement in its earlier stages. Austrian Socialism owes much to him. It should be said that Adler personally deprecates the credit he has got for his pecuniary sacrifices to the party, saying that it was not so much after all, and that too much had been made of it. In any case, however, it amounted to the best part of the fortune his father left him. Suffering for some years from asthma and chronic bronchial catarrh, Adler was in the habit, up to the outbreak of the war in 1914, of spending some two or three months of the worst part of the winter on the Riviera, where I often met him. He has, of late years especially, developed marked opportunist or, as it would be called in the German-speaking world, "Revisionist" tendencies. His belief in parliamentary action as a means for the emancipation of the proletariat is unbounded. He seems at times, indeed, to regard Socialist principles with a certain amount of impatience, as a hindrance to the party's activity in so-called "practical politics."

One of the most effective speakers amongst Austrian Socialists (Adler himself is not a good speaker) is the former Radical and veteran party politician, Engelbert Pernerstorfer. There are few men in Austria who can sway a large popular assembly with their eloquence as can Pernerstorfer.

The Austrian movement has produced many able men whom the exigencies of space preclude from particularizing. There is one, however, who, not himself a member of the Socialist party though generally sympathetic with its aims, is well known in certain circles in this country as the energetic secretary of the "International League for the Protection of Workmen," having its central bureau in Switzerland, at Basel. I refer to Stephen Bauer, who, in addition to his secretaryship of the League in question, occupies the position of Professor of Political Economy in Basel University. Bauer was a great friend of the late Sir Charles Dilke, at whose house he was a frequent visitor. His International League for Workmen's Protection, which was founded at a meeting of International delegates held at Zürich in 1897, is anything but Socialistic in its character and mode of working. It is based rather on the notion of gaining the support and assistance of the various national governments in the furtherance of its object; in a word, it relies on the official class in the various countries rather than on the democracy for the realization of its object. Still, small as may be the faith of the Socialist in any serious amelioration of the lot of the workman resulting from these methods, even he must pay a tribute to the energy of the League's secretary in waiting on ministers, under-secretaries of departments, not to speak of the smaller fry of officialdom, soliciting both personally and by letter their support and interest with their respective: governments on its behalf. And he claims to have achieved at least something. Whether this something is worth the time, energy, and machinery expended on it, and whether such might not have been used to a better purpose, is another question. Stephen Bauer is a good linguist, a brilliant conversationalist, and knows his Anglo-Saxondom, both British and American, well.

The mention of Basel reminds me of another professor (though not an Austrian) at the Basel University, a man of acute and powerful intellect, a friend and colleague of Bauer's, to wit, Robert Michels. Of an old German family of the Rhineland, Michels has lived for many years in Italy, and has, I believe, recently become a naturalized Italian. Michels began life as a German officer, but the horrors of militarism in general and of the Prusso-German military service in particular led him to renounce his original profession and take to an academic career. He soon after joined the Socialist movement, but it was not long before he became dissatisfied with the inaction and opportunism of the party as represented in the Reichstag, which he criticized, not sparing some of the honoured leaders, in more than one scathing article. During his residence in Italy, where he obtained the professorship of Political Economy at Turin, his membership of the German party seems to have lapsed. He was, however, present at the International Congress at Stuttgart in 1907. Here occurred a trifling incident which affords an illustration of a significant trait in the German national character, to wit, its excessive tendency to hero-worship. Some appreciative remarks to some of the Germans present having been made by an English delegate *à propos* of Michels, the observation came from the German side that Michels, it was understood, had written something against Bebel, the implication being that if this were so he was a man with whom one should have nothing to do. Now, Michels, in denouncing the slackness and opportunist tendencies of the Socialist party in the Reichstag, had, as a matter of fact, criticized Bebel. But there was nothing in his article of a personally offensive nature, or that was otherwise than what would elsewhere have been regarded, whether right or wrong in itself, as perfectly fair comment. But the shuddering horror at the laying of a sacrilegious hand on the party leader is, as already said, characteristic. It is only fair to Bebel to add that he himself took the matter much more sensibly, and meeting Michels in a hotel in a Swiss health resort a year or two later, became perfectly friendly.

Bebel's own good sense in the matter excited the indignation of, I am sorry to say, other Germanic colleagues, among them Victor Adler, who expressed to me the opinion that Bebel ought to have refused to speak with his critic in terms of social intercourse. I had a further illustration of this same national characteristic on Bebel's will becoming known, and this time it was again exemplified in the person of Adler. Speaking of the will, I ventured the harmless remark to Adler that I was rather surprised that Bebel had not left a larger sum to the party. I did not say this in any spirit of severe criticism or even of disapproval, but the bare remark was enough to excite Adler's indignant remonstrances, which even tended to overstep the limits of personal courtesy. Hero-worship up to a point may be an excusable and even a laudable sentiment, but hero-worship developed to the point of an idolatry which would place its object above criticism, thus making of the latter a kind of God Almighty, whose name must not be mentioned save in terms of reverential adulation, is surely to be deprecated. Adler comes, of course, of Jewish stock, but, as is often the case with the Jewish race, he has completely assimilated the characteristics and tradition of the nationality with which his family have been for so many generations identified. And the trait just referred to is, I venture to think, significant beyond what might at first sight appear. It seems peculiar to the German character and national habit – this slavish attitude towards persons in authority, whether party leaders, kings, kaisers, policemen, or non-commissioned officers. It will explain much in the somewhat abject role played by the German peoples towards their Prussian rulers in recent events. This servile strain in the German character is a strange blemish in a race otherwise possessed of such great intellectual Powers. The "cold-shouldering" of Robert Michels for criticizing Bebel by his former colleagues of the Social Democratic party is of a piece with the toleration by the German people as a whole of the laws of *lèse-majesté* and Prussian military discipline, etc.

Turning to the Italian comrades, among those I have known best are Turati, since become a somewhat moderate and chastened Socialist light of Monte-Citorio. At the time I knew him he was in association with Madame Kolischoff, a Russian lady who has played a not uninfluential part in the Italian Socialist party in earlier years. Much more intimate than with Turati was my acquaintance with that genial free-lance Paulo Valera. A clever and even brilliant journalist, Valera has never been in the Italian chamber, or has, indeed, played any very important role in the party organization itself. He is known best as pamphleteer. In this capacity and on his own lines he has scarcely an equal in Italy, though the chief seat of his activity remains local, to wit, Milan and Lombardy. Professor Enrico Ferri, whose picturesque figure of old Roman type did not fail to attract attention at Socialist Congresses, was known as a fine orator, and for a time led the left wing of the Italian movement. Of genial disposition, and socially agreeable as he was, I have always regretted his defection from his old principles. It is not so many years ago since I was one of a large number of Socialists of all countries to sign their names to an illuminated address which was presented to him as a testimony to his services for the cause.

Among the Russians, I have already in an earlier chapter spoken of Kropotkin. The late Wolkowsky was for some years well known in London political circles. He was also prominent as a lecturer on his personal experiences in the Russian movement. I heard him deliver his lecture entitled *The Story of my Life*, in which he described his persecutions at the hands of the Russian authorities, in the Temple, to the members of the Hardwicke Society. A more important person than the last mentioned was

Sergius Stepniak, whose real name was Kravchinsky. Of powerful build, thickset, and of strong Mongoloid face and figure, Stepniak was a prominent personality in advanced London society during the eighties and early nineties. I cannot recall anything especially striking in his conversation, though the man conveyed an undoubted impression of power in his whole personality. **Underground Russia** and **The Career of a Nihilist**, the latter book a novel that excited the warm admiration of Shaw, undoubtedly give evidence of literary genius, each in its own way. Stepniak's untimely death by an express train on the level crossing near Turnham Green assuredly cut short the career of one who would have achieved much more than he did had he lived.

Another personality among the advanced Russian politicians with whom I came much in contact is worthy our attention for a moment. I refer to the one time Slade Professor of Slav language and literature at Oxford, the late Maxim Kowalewski. Like most cultivated Russians, he spoke fluently, besides his native tongue, English, German, French, and Italian. Though not himself a professed Socialist, Kowalewski was on terms of personal friendship with many of the leading representatives of Socialist thought throughout Europe. Marx and Engels he knew well and was much liked by them. Vandervelde was also a friend of Kowalewski and a frequent visitor at his villa in Beaulieu, besides other more or less prominent members of the Socialist party. Speaking for myself, I shall always have pleasant recollections of the hospitality received at the Villa Batava. Kowalewski had a man servant or valet of local origin named Baptiste, but who was colloquially spoken of as "Leporello," of whom he used to relate amusing anecdotes. On applying for the situation, this worthy gave as one of his qualifications that he had received the first prize for dancing in his native village. On one occasion when Kowalewski was about to give a large dinner-party, he duly instructed "Leporello," when serving at table, to help the older ladies before the younger ones. "Leporello" endeavoured conscientiously to carry out his master's instructions. Now it so happened there were two ladies sitting near each other, alike of doubtful and uncertain age. Accordingly, our "Leporello," not quite knowing which to serve first, decided to solve the matter by putting the question straight to them, *"Mesdames, laquelle de vous est la plus anciennes?"* During the latter years of his life Kowalewski resided in Russia, where, probably as a sop thrown to the left wing of the Duma, he was offered a seat on the Russian Imperial Council. He accepted it, he told me, when he called on me a year or two ago on a flying visit to his old haunts, thinking he might bring successful pressure to bear on the Government in favour of political prisoners. This seems actually to have been the case in some instances.

Before closing the present chapter it may be worth while to say a few words on the general subject of International Congresses. The first of the series of International Socialist Congresses, which were interrupted by the outbreak of the European War, though not before they had resulted in the establishment of the International Bureau, thereby constituting the New International, as it was called, was held in 1889 in Paris. At this Congress, which divided itself into two, owing to the split between the Guesdist and the Broussist sections of the French party, I was not present. A second Congress was held two years later at Brussels, in which I also took no part. The third Congress was at Zürich in 1893, and on this occasion I attended as a delegate of the Social Democratic Federation. This Congress was notable for the fact that Friedrich Engels made the closing speech, in the course of which he explained the reasons for the action of Marx and himself which led to the break-up of the old International in the seventies. The reasons given, as I have already stated, were that they both felt that the organization in its then existing form had done its work, and that it was not strong enough to face the opposition and persecution with which it was threatened by the Governments of Europe. They felt, he said, that its continued existence at that time was likely only to result in unnecessary suffering for members of the working-class movement, and perhaps even the loss of some of its best leaders. This authoritative statement made by Engels has undoubtedly considerable interest for the historian of the Socialist party, although the point of view taken might have, and has indeed, been traversed by those not belonging to the Marxian section in the narrower sense in which the Fre-tch used to speak of "la chapelle Marx." For the rest, the Zürich Congress of 1893 was signalized by some disturbances created by the Anarchist and quasi-Anarchist elements that had got into certain of the delegations, especially the French and the Dutch.

Up to the Zürich Congress these meetings had been held every two years, as decided by the Paris Congress of 1889. But at Zürich the German party pressed for a longer interval between the International gatherings, suggesting even four or five years as not too long. Eventually three years was decided upon, and the next Congress took place in 1896 in London. It was held at the Queen's Hall, and I was elected on to the Standing Orders Committee. The Congress opened noisily, owing to the intrusion of Anarchist elements. The French delegation had stormy sittings and eventually became split into two parts, the moderate section of which Millerand was a member refusing to work any longer with the extreme section. The latter section, if not actually Anarchist, certainly had Anarchistic tendencies, though its opponents, it is only fair to say, included men like Millerand himself, whose Socialist principles were unquestionably of a very doubtful character. At this Congress measures were taken for the exclusion of Anarchists and, as far as possible, other disturbing elements from future Congresses.

The next Congress was held in Paris in 1900, at the time of the Exhibition. It was due in 1899, but the German party, having failed to secure officially a longer term than three years for the interval between the Congresses, obtained by intrigue behind the scenes a prolongation of a year. The same tactics were adopted by the German party on more than one subsequent occasion. The chief feature of the Paris Congress of 1900 was the dissension between the sections of the French party, which had as its result a defective organization of the arrangements. In consequence the gathering, although well attended, was not as successful as some others have been.

I may mention that, the week immediately preceding the Paris Congress of 1900, the German party held its own Congress at Mainz, at which I was also present. Here I made the interesting acquaintance of the Kapellmeister and composer Weissheimer, who was a friend of Wagner and is referred to with, for him, an unusual appreciation in his autobiography. Weissheimer, who conducted the opera at Mainz for many years, was a member of the Social Democratic party and took part in the Congress. At the close of the proceedings one evening, in reply to a question of mine respecting the best place to obtain genuine Rhenish wine, Weissheimer took us to a special *Weinstube* that he knew of, when more than one flagon of "Rhenish" was consumed – in fact, more perhaps than a stern moralist in these matters like my friend Hyndman would have approved. Weissheimer, I remember, was particularly pleased when I told him that Felix Moscheles, the son of Ignaz Moscheles, the celebrated pianist, by whom he had been taught in his youth, was, if not a declared Socialist, at least a Democrat, an Internationalist, and a strong anti-militarist.

A very interesting Congress was that held at Amsterdam in 1904 (the Germans having again succeeded in postponing it for a year). It was on this occasion that the question of opportunism and the taking part by members of the Socialist Party in current politics was discussed, with the results already- spoken of in the unification of the French party. The debates at this Congress issued in the passing of resolutions condemning the participation of Socialists officially in existing State governments, and generally in "*bourgeois* politics." The Congress held at Stuttgart in 1907 was memorable for the expulsion of Quelch from Würtemberg for his characterization of the diplomatic conference, then sitting at The Hague, on the peace question, as a "thieves' supper." It was also remarkable for the strong stand made by Gustave Hervé on the question of patriotism and national military organization – the same Hervé who is now so enthusiastic a patriot.

If we except the special Peace Congress called at Basel on the outbreak of the Balkan War, the last International Socialist Congress was that held at Copenhagen in 1910. Here also the question of armaments and peace was largely to the fore, but in general the gathering, though successful in every way as a Congress, the arrangements of the Danish comrades having been altogether excellent, was not distinguished by any special features. The following Congress should have taken place at Vienna in 1913, but this time once more the German party insisted on having it put off for a year. All arrangements had been made for holding the gathering in Vienna in August of the fateful year 1914, but the great world catastrophe intervened, and International Socialism was deprived of the possibility of making a united pronouncement on the question of international relations generally, and of the special circumstances that had led up to the European situation as it then stood in particular. This is much to be regretted, since had the Congress been held in 1913 according to the instructions given to the International Bureau at Copenhagen, the probabilities are it would have resulted at least in the clearing of the air on the general question of war, and on the attitude of the various Socialist parties towards it, in the event of hostilities arising. I know it maybe said that in general terms the question had already been dealt with at previous Congresses, but the terms were too general. Moreover, in the three years that had elapsed since the last Congress, that at Copenhagen, the international situation had considerably changed, and in a sense undeniably rendering essential a more detailed and more precise pronouncement on the eventuality of a great European war, for determining the practical attitude of the party on this all-important question.

# VII. Literary Work

In writing these reminiscences, I have, as already stated in the preface, made it a rule to damp down the personal note as far as possible, and to avoid the example of Lord Herbert of Cherbury of giving prominence to my own valiant deeds. But, seeing they are after all personal reminiscences, it would seem out of place, and even pedantic, to suppress altogether all account of the individual reminiscencer's achievements, such as they are and what there are of them. In the present chapter, therefore, I am going frankly to talk about myself, so those not interested may pass it over. But what I have to chronicle I should premise are no glorious deeds of valour, but resolve themselves simply into a little modest literary work.

My first excursions into the regions of print consisted in a few articles in obscure monthlies devoted to natural history, a subject on which at the time, being then in my early teens, I was very keen. It was some few years before I produced anything more. My next piece of literary output, so far as I can recollect, was in 1876, and was a result of my studies on the French Revolution, namely a little book in vindication of Jean Paul Marat. I returned to this subject, I should say, over twenty years later at the suggestion of my friend Mr. Grant Richards, who published a life of Marat by me in the nineties of the last century. About the time of my first sketch of Marat's life an article from my pen on the subject appeared in the **Gentleman's Magazine**. Barring articles in periodicals and newspapers, as also the episode of my newspaper correspondentship in Berlin alluded to in an earlier chapter, my next literary effort was a translation of Kant's **Prolegomena to all Future Metaphysic** and his **Metaphysical Foundations of Natural Science**, with a life of Kant and an introduction to the **Critical philosophy** prefixed, the latter occupying about a third of the whole volume, which was published in *Bohn's Philosophical Library*. Thus was followed a year or two later by my **Handbook of the History of Philosophy**, also in the same series, a book which was very well received and had a considerable success, as works on philosophy go, with the British public. Later on I published with the same firm (Messrs. Bell and Sons) a translation of a selection from Schopenhauer's **Parerga and Paralipomena** under the title of **Schopenhauer's Essays**, preceded by a life of Schopenhauer and a critical exposition of his philosophy.

It was about the middle eighties that I began the publication of a sequence of popular works on Socialism for Messrs. Sonnenschein & Co.'s *Social Science Series*. The first of them was **The Religion of Socialism**, consisting of essays dealing with various aspects of Socialism. These, of course, are now a generation old, and, addressed as they were to a public of over thirty years ago, their point of view and expression naturally may strike the reader of the present day as not being quite up to date. As to this, while maintaining in full the essential principles put forward in these earlier essays, I am prepared, of course, to admit that there are some things which from the present-day standpoint may appear over-emphasized, while there are others either omitted or from the same standpoint insufficiently elaborated. I already acknowledge this in my preface to the fifth edition (1901). And what I said then applies, of course, still more to-day. But the book has passed through so many editions that it may well be left as it is – always, of course, on the assumption that in essentials it still expresses the views of the author. The success of the **Religion of Socialism** led to the production of other books of a similar character and scope by myself and others. In fact, it practically gave a send-off to the *Social Science Series*.[1] My own next contribution was the **Ethics of Socialism**, the success of which was almost, if not quite, equal to that of the **Religion of Socialism**, notwithstanding the fact that it was not, as in the former case, exclusively concerned with Socialism, containing three rather important essays on other subjects. Following this appeared a third volume of similar character

130

entitled **Outlooks from the New Standpoint**. This book had a fairly good sale, although, curiously enough, not nearly equal to that of the two former, in spite of the fact that it contained essays dealing with subjects more "topical" than either of them. During the anniversary years of the French Revolution I contributed my **Story of the French Revolution** to the same series. A little later I wrote for the Twentieth Century Press a short history of the Commune of Paris of 1871. This little book, though scarcely more than a brochure, is, I believe, the only history of the Commune within the same compass in the English language. It was based largely on Lissagaray's exhaustive work on the subject. It is satisfactory to know that it circulated widely amongst English Socialists. The same may be said of a pamphlet entitled **A New Catechism of Socialism**, in which my late friend Harry Quelch and myself collaborated. The allusion in the title was to an old pamphlet published at the beginning of the English movement by J.L. Joynes called **Socialist Catechism**, now out of print. Our own brochure, consisting of some forty-four pages, was published by the Twentieth Century Press at twopence, and has had a circulation of many thousands.

The nineties saw the successive publication of my three volumes on the social side of the Reformation in Germany, bearing the respective titles of **German Society at the Close of the Middle Ages**, **The Peasants' War**, and **The Rise and Fall of the Anabaptists**. These three volumes contain an exhaustive history of certain sides of the Reformation period in Central Europe, such as is not to be found otherwise, I may venture to say, in the whole range of English historical literature. But although well reviewed, they never attained a second edition. Purely historical literature, like purely philosophical literature, has apparently no great public among the reading population of the British Islands, except where it connects itself with some popular interest of the day or some problem which happens to have come temporarily into prominence.

Shortly before the appearance of the first of the volumes

131

last mentioned I published, also with Messrs, Sonnenschein, a small philosophical work entitled **The Problem of Reality**, containing in a brief sketch suggestions for a philosophical reconstruction. This little book, while its theses were based on philosophic Idealism generally, was opposed to the current neo-Hegelian position, which was at that time still paramount in English philosophy. About the same time I published another small volume, entitled **Outspoken Essays**, dealing with historical and social subjects. During these early years of the nineties I also collaborated with the late William Morris in the work we entitled **Socialism, its Growth and Outcome**, which was also published (as a double volume) in Sonnenschein's *Social Science Series*. It claims to be a history of the development of the Socialistic idea, in its practical aspects, beginning with primitive Communism, tracing the decay of the communistic group system and the rise of Individualism, economical and otherwise, and the various fluctuations throughout history in respect to these two principles, leading up to the modern Socialist movement, as embodying consciously Socialism as the ideal of the future. The book, although it had a fair sale, has not passed without criticism from various sides. That it has its defects and weak points may be true, but I still contend that, taken as a whole, it is as adequate a statement of a big subject as could be compressed into the same compass.

About this time I was called to the Bar at the Middle Temple, which I had joined some three years before. For a year or two after this I had some notion of actively following the legal profession, and took steps in that direction, but subsequently abandoned the idea. My time was thus left free for other studies and literary work. Continuing my record with regard to the latter, the new life of Marat already referred to was written at the end of the nineties, and reached a second edition two or three years after its publication. Early in the new century a volume of mixed contents was published by Grant Richard, under the title **Essays in Socialism Old and New**. It comprised most of the pieces contained in the **Outspoken Essays**, which had appeared some ten years earlier and had gone out of print, and a number of new pieces. The above was followed by what I personally regard as my most important literary production, to wit, **The Roots of Reality**. This book was based upon the conclusions put forward tentatively some years previously in the brief sketch before alluded to, **The Problem of Reality**. The positions these laid down are in the later and much larger volume developed, corrected, and added to, and other problems dealt with. It is now out of print and awaiting a second and enlarged edition on the conclusion of the present war; but as it stands, it labours under the disadvantage that its criticism of the Hegelian, or, as I have termed it, the "pallogistic" position in philosophy, is disproportionately emphasized in view of the fact of the changes that have taken place during the last ten years in the general outlook of speculative thought in this country. "Pragmatism," Bergson, and other influences quite foreign and even opposed to the Hegelian Pallogism or Intellectualism (as it is some times called), have since become fashionable, and from the point of view of **The Roots of Reality** call for a special criticism of their own, There are also other suggestions I have received as regards presentment and illustration, to the intent to render the positions advanced more readily understandable of the lay reader, and these also demand serious consideration in the revised edition, which the writer hopes in due time will see the light.

After **The Roots of Reality** had appeared, I bethought me of a promise to my old friend William Morris, made not long before his death, to write a history of that, even to most students, little-known event at the close of the French Revolution, Gracchus Babeuf's "Conspiracy of the Equals." This undertaking I now endeavoured to fulfil to the best of my ability, and the result was the volume entitled **The Last Episode of the French Revolution** (Grant Richard), which appeared in 1911. The book, though well enough reviewed, had the sale one expects from purely historical monographs having little or no bearing on current events or practical interest for the present time. It remains, however, as the only English study on the subject obtainable, even Bronterre O'Brien's translation of the contemporary Buonarotti's work having been out of print for more than half a century.

This was followed in 1912 by another volume of essays, entitled **Essays on Men, Mind, and Morals**, comprising some previously published and some unpublished pieces, among the former the article that originally appeared in the **International Journal of Ethics** on the Socialist view of the fundamental principles of morality, and my reply in the **Fortnightly Review** to Dr. Beattie Crozier's attack on Socialism. In November 1913 appeared **The Fraud of Feminism**, just after Sir Almroth Wright's **Unexpurgated Case against Woman Suffrage**. In this little book of less than two hundred pages I claim to have disposed of the arguments (save the mark!), so constantly heard and so seldom contradicted or refuted, of the advocates of Feminism. I have clearly drawn the distinction between Political Feminism (as I have termed it) and Sentimental Feminism. The Political Feminist claims for women equal political and social rights with men. The Sentimental Feminist, under the sham pretence of chivalry, claims impunity for women from the unpleasant consequences of their own conduct. Between the two, and they are usually combined in the same person, we arrive at the delightful conclusion that women have a right to claim an equal position with men wherever it suits their book, i.e. in all honourable, agreeable, and lucrative positions, and at the same time to demand special treatment from that accorded to men whenever "equality" would spell unpleasant consequences for themselves – a charming doctrine truly for the female sex, in which the "equality" appears with its picturesque chivalry "all on one side."

My efforts in this book, as in previous essays, to expose the claptrap and lies of the advocates of Feminism have naturally not been to the taste of the Suffragette sisterhood, who have lost

134

no opportunity of venting their petty spite in feeble efforts to say nasty things. I give just one instance of this. In the Spring of 1915 appeared a volume called forth by the war, entitled **German Culture, Past and Present**.[2] It consisted largely of excerpts from my previous volumes on the social side of the Reformation in Germany, with two concluding chapters on Modern Germany. The book was very favourably received by the Press generally, but there was one dissentient voice in a certain London morning daily of strong Feminist tendencies, wherein appeared a notice in which every one detected the hand of the Suffragette. The lady in question, who, of course, wrote under the veil of anonymity, headed her article *Mr. Bax **in extremis**!* (she probably meant *in excelsis!*). After a few words of general attack on the ground that all the contents were not new, she proceeded to single out and quote from the last chapter a couple of plain-sailing English sentences, upon which she pronounced her *ipse dixit* that the style was "bad" and the thought "jejune." Now, what does the reader think these two "bad" and "jejune" sentences purported to say? Simply that in the humble judgment of the author the influence of the writings of Nietzsche on Modern Germany was not as powerful as some writers on the war had represented. Of course, I may have been wrong in my view as to this, but I submit that to describe such an opinion, whether right or wrong, precisely as "jejune" indicates a singular ignorance of the correct use of the English language as possible with advanced womanhood. As a matter of fact, these last two chapters of the book in question were written somewhat hurriedly, and in consequence one or two real if trivial errors had crept into them, which, unimportant as they were in themselves, were such as in the hands of a skilful critic bent on being "nasty" might (especially in a short notice) have been effectively exploited against me. These, however, my female critic had evidently neither the brains nor the knowledge to take advantage of. Accordingly, the foolish young woman who aimed at smartness achieved silliness.

This incident, which might hardly seem worthy of

mention in itself, is nevertheless otherwise significant inasmuch as it betrays a type of mental attitude prevalent in the younger present generation, and especially in the youthful "emancipated" female. It is the morbid craving after literary fireworks – the dread of the commonplace become a disease. Every sentence that does not wrap up an epigram, every expression of opinion that does not wear the air of a paradox, is voted dull and vapid. These fatuous would-be up-to-date young prigs seem, moreover, oblivious of the everyday fact that it is often necessary in controversy and otherwise to remind an opponent, or even the casual reader, of what ought to be obvious. There are plenty of people, for that matter, with whom it is necessary on occasion to call their attention to the fact that two and two make four. But, even apart from this, the demand of priggish up-to-datism that every paragraph, if it is to be worth the trouble of reading, must enshrine an uninterrupted series of epigrams or paradoxes, is silly and insufferable. In fact, the overdoing of the epigrammatic and paradoxical may very easily run to seed in a claptrap and a banality of its own. As pointed out in an earlier chapter, it may fairly be doubted whether Shaw, able man though he is, does not sometimes overshoot the mark in this respect. Talking of Shaw reminds me, by the way, of an incident bearing on the above. On my remarking to Shaw one day that our mutual friend J.L. Joynes had observed to me that he should not particularly care to have him for a companion in a long tour, Shaw replied, "Well, I can't reciprocate the sentiment, for I think Joynes would suit me very well as a travelling companion; but I know what he meant: I dare say I should be always trying to say smart things, and this after a time might tend to become boresome." So it is. Excessive wit may weary, just as excessive sweetness may satiate. If there is but one step from the sublime to the ridiculous, there are likewise not many steps from the brilliant to the banal. And the steps are counted in the overloading of writing or discourse with points and effects – and this however good these may be in themselves.

As regards my literary activity, I have always been at the

disadvantage of not having the faculty possessed by many of expanding a subject I am writing upon indefinitely. I have the scheme of what I conceive to be essential in the exposition of my subject, and I write up to it. But I have a difficulty in filling out beyond this to meet the exigencies of printers and publishers. The above is an undoubted drawback, since the dilution of one's subject with words and style is what in many cases the public wants. On the other hand, the facility in reeling out verbal material has its disadvantages even in historical writing, although not nearly so much as in philosophical. Even where the material is not purely verbal, but to a large extent real, there is always a danger of overweighting, so that the reader is apt to get into the position of not being able to see the wood for the trees. The salient points which are essential are apt to get confused in a mass of relatively, and sometimes more than relatively, unimportant detail. The observance of proportion in the subject matter of serious work, though obviously an essential in all such writing, is as often as not failed of attainment even with men of ability. In historical writing it is exceedingly difficult to steer between the Scylla of bareness and sketchiness and the Charybdis of overweighting with incidental material, which leaves confusion as to the general import of events in the mind of the reader. This applies, of course, more to popular historical writing than to works of scholarship designed for students, where a certain amount of overweighting is scarcely avoidable. Of the latter class of work Gibbon is supposed to be the model in this respect. But it may fairly be doubted whether Gibbon's handling of his material in the **Decline and Fall**, as regards proportion, is not excelled by Hodgson in his **Invaders of Italy**.

Where, however, the reeling out of an immense mass of verbal product is most dangerous to effectiveness is in highly abstract subjects, especially philosophy. Here diffuseness is absolutely fatal to the leaving of any strong impression on the mind of the reader. This is especially noticeable in certain American writers, notably Professor Baldwin, whose three volumes **Thought and Things** are devoted to material which on a liberal computation might easily be got into one. Other American writers of philosophical treatises are guilty of the same indiscretion, to wit, of drowning the essentials of their thought in portentous volumes of closely printed pages which look imposing but leave little impression on the reader. In philosophy, more than in anything else, it is desirable to avoid diffuseness and overexpansion, not only by mere verbiage, but by the introduction of a mass of detail and discussion of fifth-rate problems on the fringe of the main subject. One sometimes finds this over, elaboration in works of real genius and even of epoch making character. For example, the **Kapital** of Marx is not wholly free therefrom. It is, indeed, more particularly noticeable in the posthumous second and third volume, although, especially as regards the third volume, since it was left by its author in a condition of notes and jottings merely, it would be manifestly unfair to saddle these shortcomings altogether on Marx himself.

Returning to my own literary work, I may mention that it has been my fortune to have what we are told is the sincerest form of flattery, namely, imitation, more than once practised upon me. The authors who have done this have at the same time been careful not to acknowledge the source of their indebtedness. Thus a year or so after the publication of my little sketch **The Problem of Reality** appeared a work by an eminent British statesman of philosophic pretensions, which contained a criticism of the Hegelian Pallogism, especially with reference to its modern expressions in the works of Thomas Hill Green and others, which was practically identical with my own. Conclusions arrived at independently, the reader will say! Possibly, but the similarity of the argument, and even of its expression, seemed singularly close, and for me the more significant in view of the fact that I had some grounds for believing the distinguished philosophic statesman in question might not have been altogether without knowledge of my own humble and insignificant effort.

Again, in the works of a well-known popular essayist I

could point to paragraphs which are almost identical reproductions of passages of my own. Another well-known writer on social and economic subjects, in a work of his published a year or two ago, devotes a long final chapter to the elaboration, without acknowledgment, of my speculation as to the evolution of a social consciousness presented in **The Roots of Reality** (pp.126-36). I am not making a personal grievance out of these things, but I may say that as a general principle I cannot approve of the literary morality which does not hesitate to "lift" ideas, and in some cases even turns of expression, from an isolated thinker, a thing no one would dare to do in the case of a man holding an academic chair or otherwise very much in the public view. In the first case the "lifting" may pass unobserved; in the second, those who practised it would be likely to be "dropped upon" at once.

An amusing, because so flagrant, a case of the false attribution of an idea in the interest apparently of the academic "guild" in general is the cool reference by a distinguished American professor of philosophy of the term "alogical," in the sense in which I have used it, to Professor Bergson. Professor Bergson himself, who, in spite of his eminence in the world of modern philosophic thought, is personally the most modest of men, told me in conversation that, while approving of my use of the word, he had not seen it, certainly in the sense used by me, before he read **The Roots of Reality**.

All I have to say upon this question of property in ideas is that if the provenance of ideas or literary expression is to be acknowledged at all, it should be acknowledged equally all round without distinction of persons. To acknowledge, perhaps with effusiveness, indebtedness for a thought when its author holds a professorship or is prominently before the public eye in other ways, and to reproduce a thought without a word of acknowledgment of its source where its author holds no distinguished post or is generally less in the public view, I think it will be admitted by most impartial persons savours of a certain degree of meanness. Yet there seems to be a notion abroad that the works of such a one may be used as an open quarry and their contained ideas fully appropriated, the original author being conveniently ignored.

Setting aside the purely philosophical issues discussed in **The Roots of Reality**, which are too technical to be entered into at length in a book of this nature, some readers might be inclined to ask what I consider as my special contribution to modern thought on the subjects on which I have written. It is difficult to answer this question satisfactorily. But among the few small services my work may have helped is the calling attention to the distinction between the morality of early society, with its basis of communal or group feeling and thinking, and the introspective morality, sometimes called the Ethics of Inwardness, based on the individual and his relation as a spiritual being, considered more or less *per se*, to a deity who is the supreme power of the Universe. In the first case the basis of morality and religion is custom and traditionally prescribed action or ritual, the question of individual motive hardly entering into it; the second, the inner motives and feelings of the individual occupy the foremost place. I think I may claim, without pretending to be the actual protagonist of this idea, to which modern anthropology has been leading up for many years, to have been the first popularly to emphasize the distinction in connexion with the light it throws upon the doctrine and aspirations of the socialism of to-day. The distinction between the communal thought or feeling by which the man was absolutely merged in the group-clan, tribe, or people – before individuality or logical thought, in our sense, had arisen; and that of civilization, which meant, as one of its chief features, the development of the individual as such, and his freeing from the ties and order of ideas which identified him with the group under earlier conditions of society, it was always my endeavour to impress upon the thinking section of Socialists and of those interested in social problems. This point, that I have since a generation ago, in a bare and, I willingly admit, inadequate form, endeavoured to popularize among my contemporaries, has of late

140

years, with perhaps certain modifications and on a more extended scale, been worked out from another side in a most original manner and with considerable learning by the new Cambridge school of anthropologists. The fact that classical scholarship has largely been employed to this end, and the evolution of ancient Greek society taken as typical, I hold to be no disadvantage, but rather the contrary. Useful and indeed indispensable as the comparative method of the investigation of the conditions of existing savage and barbaric communities may be, Greece nevertheless lies in the main stream of human evolution, and must therefore, with the other self-evolving civilized races of the ancient world, represent the type of social progress in a manner which the existing survivals of early society in outlying parts of the world do not. The latter may be compared to eddies and side-streams of the main course of human development, which do not necessarily represent in their present conditions the exact counterpart of any past phase in the evolution of the historic races, however much they may afford us illustrations of, and clues to, the general course of that evolution.

There are plenty of other points which I have endeavoured to bring out in my literary work. The above I only give as a specimen of an important one. I am aware that I have the misfortune, for the rest, while able perhaps sometimes to throw out ideas worthy of consideration, in a bare and sketchy manner, to lack the equally necessary capacity of working them out in detail and thereby demonstrating their truth. I am perfectly willing to admit this as a defect; whether a defect of my qualities must depend upon the decision of others and the public generally as to whether I have any. with this observation I may fairly conclude the present, I trust not too long, chapter on my own literary doings and sufferings.

## Notes

1. Now published by George Allen & Unwin Ltd.

2. George Allen & Unwin Ltd.

# VIII. Club And Temple Life in London at the End of the Nineteenth Century

The decades of the nineties has already receded from us sufficiently to become interesting as a retrospect. Though the change in English thought and ways of looking at life, as regards what had gone before it, was not nearly so profound or far-reaching as that the early eighties had to show, yet the nineties had none the less a character of their own. The ideas and movements which had struck root in the eighties were growing up and sprouting out in various directions, but it is less with the intellectual than with the social life of that period that I propose to deal in this chapter.

In the course of the year 1889 I joined a well-known club[1] in the West End of London, and the following year I took up my residence in the Temple, as already mentioned in an earlier chapter. The club I joined was a large one, with a membership embracing all sorts and conditions of men. Moreover, it was a political club, and included at that time men who have since played prominent part in the public life of the country. Journalists not unnaturally bulked largely among the membership. Men of law, some of them not wanting in eminence, were also among the habitues of the smoking room. Living as I was by myself in chambers at the time[2], as is the wont in such cases, I tended to drift into the club during the latter part of the day. Here I mixed with the other habitual frequenters, among whom there were some noteworthy types which have not failed to impress themselves upon my memory. There was a barrister with a sufficiently good practice who got the credit of being remiss in the matter of standing drinks. This reminds me, by the way, of one notable difference which twenty odd years have made in one at least of the social customs of club-life. In the early nineties, giving and accepting of alcoholic refreshment played a much greater part in the social intercourse of club smoking-rooms, as indeed it did also in life outside clubs, than it does nowadays. No one who remembers the time, even as late as that referred to, can fail to appraise at its true value the cant which declaims against drink as being the special curse of the England of to-day. Even from twenty to twenty-five years ago there was at least twice as much alcohol consumed as there was, let us say, in the summer of 1914, i.e. before the special war restrictions on liquor came into force. If we go farther back, of course, the difference is still more striking. The days depicted by Dickens in **Pickwick** are astounding to the modern man.

But to return to the club. There was the youngish gentleman, undergraduate of the London University, who did a little journalism and acted on occasion as electoral agent and canvasser for party candidates whom he approved. Having a little means of his own, he did this work for the most part gratuitously. A constant inmate of the club at this time, he was a well-known character. Especially was he famous for the air of blaseness and ennui which he usually assumed. The idea ever present in his mind appeared to be that to seem bored was rather "tony". Hence the idea of boredom occupied a considerable place in his thought. It was in vain I pointed out to him that excessive sensitiveness to bores and boredom had never been a characteristic of the greatest minds; that, on the contrary, it was usually the mark of a mind without resilience and without formative power of its own. The really great mind, save under great provocation, is, generally speaking, tolerant in this respect, and certainly above being bored by every commonplace man it meets. The idea of boredom still remained an obsession of this gentleman. It was not so much that he was bored as that he thought he ought to appear bored.

Another among the characters of the club was the middle-aged Irish doctor, staunch patriot and ardent Catholic, with somewhat uncouth manners, who was given to laying down the law on all questions. He was generally regarded as somewhat of a crank, and not the least by his own countrymen. There were also among the members those of the House of Israel, the mention of

144

which fact recalls a humorous sally of a well-known member of the present Parliament, recently knighted. The incident was as follows: The gentleman in question was in conversation one day in the smoking-room with a barrister of the Jewish race. Sitting in a group not far off was an elderly club-member, since dead, who in loud tones was heard to express the opinion that there were too many of "these damn'd Jews" in the club. The remark, of course, had no reference to the Jewish gentleman with whom our MP was speaking, whose presence a short distance off had probably not been observed by our anti-Semitic friend. However, it reached the ears of the former, whose indignation was at once aroused to the extent of his getting up and going over to remonstrate with the insulter, as he deemed him, of his racial colleagues in the club, whose remarks he took as a personal affront to himself. In altercation ensued on the merits of the Hebrew, which was threatening to become hot, when our MP interposed with the observation that he thought the whole difference between his friend and the old gentleman was due to a misunderstanding; if he had heard aright, he understood the latter's objection to refer, not to Jews in general either within or without the club, but only a special class of Jews, to wit, *damm'd* Jews. "Now," he said, "we none of us approve of *damm'd* Jews." His friend the speaker had expressed the opinion that there were some of this class of Jew in the club. If there were, he would be the last to defend them, but although he had numerous acquaintances among the Jewish members of the club, he could not recall a single "damn'd Jew" among them. Therefore he hoped that the gentleman whose observation had given offence to his Jewish friend might have spoken from hearsay and be mistaken in his opinion. Thus the oil of humorous banter was poured on the troubled waters of anti-Semitism. Another Jewish club-story. A member of unmistakably Hebrew physiognomy, but who objected to be affiché as a Jew in the smoking-room, was present when one of the *chasseurs* was calling out as "wanted" the name of Mr. Solomon Isaacs. The member in question was evidently not there, as no response came, but the boy, zealous in the execution of his duty, seeing our friend of the Hebrew countenance sitting with his circle in a corner of the room, went up to him and addressed him, "Are you Mr. Isaacs, sir?" "No, boy; do you take me for a bloody Jew?" retorted the irate son of Israel. This anecdote illustrates the curious objection many members of the Jewish race have to acknowledge their racial origin, which may possibly have something to do with the fact that in all countries the Jew is the most aggressive patriot and jingo for his adopted or acquired nationality which that country can boast. In every nation the Jew is to be found on the side of the most fire-eating section of national chauvinists.

As I have above said, the journalist fraternity bulked largely in the membership of my club. Now, it is very curious to observe the type of mentality which work on the daily Press seems to attract, or develop, or possibly both. The pressman, while seldom a scholar or a man of depth of knowledge or of thought, is yet seldom ignorant or stupid. The intelligence of the average man of Fleet Street is aptly covered by the word "smart." He is a promiscuous gatherer of knowledge as he goes through life, as distinguished from the systematic student. The conditions of his working career of course lead to this-partly, at least; partly also there is no doubt the profession of journalism attracts to itself men of an alert type of mind, whose interests are easily awakened to almost any subject, but who are yet without either the depth or the range which is the result of intellectual staying Power. Of course, there are exceptions. There are men of scholarly type and scholarly attainments in the ranks of journalism on the one side, as there are men of crass ignorance and dullness on the other. But as a rule the successful journalist, the journalist who gets plenty to do and makes his way in the profession, is neither of the one nor the other, but a man who has the capacity for getting up any subject at command to the extent which is necessary to dilate upon it without making gross blunders, and with ail air of authority suggesting untold reserves of knowledge behind. This is very noticeable when one takes up

146

the books written by journalists. I have known men who have spoken to me on certain departments of general history, or on the histories of special countries, and who showed by their questions that the subject was quite new to them, and that in fact their knowledge concerning it was of the most elementary kind, and yet who a few months afterwards produced a book which professed glibly to instruct the public on the matter as though from the chair of a university. The man who can do this is the type of the successful journalist. Nevertheless, as above remarked, while you have on the one hand the exceptional journalist who is also a scholar and a man of depth as well as width of thought and reading, you have also on the other the exceptional pressman of elementary ignorance. A specimen of the latter, when the Moroccan question was to the fore, some few years ago, seriously asked me whether Morocco was north or south of Spain! This man, *bien entendu*, did not belong to the much despised tribe of mere reporters, but was an accredited pressman connected with a reputable London "daily"! Now, all these types of the great profession were represented in my club at the time to which this chapter specially refers, and many a pleasant hour have I spent in their Society

Amongst the men who added distinction to the club was a well-known author of books on English economic history, an Oxford professor and member of Parliament, long since dead; also two eminent authorities on Roman Law, one of them is no longer living, and the other is still a member of the club, and not only living, but working hard at intervals on an edition of an early Greek text of the Justinian Institutes, with all the careful industry of a Scottish man of learning. I should not omit to mention also the distinguished-looking member of the clerical profession, the author of a popular but none the less scholarly work on Romano-Jewish history. He is one of the widest-read men on the subject of early Christian antiquities that I know, the other two being a Privy Councillor, the author of numerous works on the origin and early history of Christianity, also a member of

147

the club, and Mr. Joseph McCabe (not a member), whose labours in this direction are equally famous. But it would be impossible to recall all the men of eminence in their several departments who have been members of the club in question. It is a club which, without claiming to be in any way "select" in the ordinary sense of the word, admirably does the work of a clearing-house for a considerable variety of men of political, social, and intellectual aims and interests of diverse character. Its catholicity in the types of its membership has always given, and does still give, occasion to the enemy to blaspheme or at least to speak disrespectfully of it as of a haunt of the philistine. Nevertheless, as I contend, it has from the beginning served, and still serves, a useful and perhaps unique purpose in the life of modern London.

Life in the Temple in the decade of the nineties the time, that is, when I was residing there, had a well-marked character of its own. The Middle Temple which was my Inn, with its old Elizabethan Hall and relics, its Vandyke Charles the First, its silver tankard for loving-cup, its snuff-box made of the wood of the Armada, as alleged, has an unfailing charm for most of its members. When I way there, there was an aged butler, such as might have made a figure for Dickens or Thackeray. Many were the stories told of this worthy and of his ways and means of enriching himself at the expense of the members. Some Middle Templers may recall his celebrated "old beer," of which by some means or other he had acquired a special cask, and which he used on occasion to dole out to the various "messes" after dinner in Hall. It was certainly the finest English ale that I have ever tasted. This curious human relic, whose object in life seemed to be perquisites, had been connected throughout his career with the legal profession, as servant to judges, as almoner in the Inns of Court, or what not. He regarded himself, as was very evident from his bearing and conversation, as an essential, if humble, limb of the law. He is now long dead, and the memory of him has probably begun to fade among the frequenters of the Middle Temple Hall.

Few of the men who haunted the precincts of the Middle Temple in the nineties are to be found there now. Twenty years have left their mark on the Temple as elsewhere. The jealousies between the briefless and the briefed doubtless continue, though the human material changes. From among the numerous barristers whom I encountered during my residence in the Temple, one or two have impressed themselves upon my memory from their having come to a tragic and untimely end. There was poor Aeneas Macintosh – as the name implies, of Scottish Highland descent - who was originally intended for the Army, but who left the military career on a point of conscience after reading Spielhagen's novel, **Problematische Naturen**, and took to the Bar. In him was present the type of the traditional Highland gentleman. He was courageous, of marked courtesy of manner, with a strong touch of old Highland Keltic superstition. I remember that after the death of a girl with whom he had had to do, he was troubled, or at least impressed, with the visits of a black cat to the window-sill of his bedroom on successive mornings, and was evidently disposed to connect the black cat in an occult manner with the deceased girl. He worked hard as a barrister, and at one time had a fair practice, but some years later, for reasons of health, he went to Canada, where he was buried in a snowdrift and never seen or heard of again.

Another Kelt, this time an Irishman and a man of a very different mould from the last mentioned, whom I saw much of during the last years of my residence at the Temple, was Michael Farelly, an amiable, feckless, thriftless person. He was always financially more or less on his beam-ends. Never very successful in his practice at the Bar, Farelly emigrated to South Africa some two or three years before the Boer War broke out. He seems to have played a somewhat doubtful role in the events which preceded the war. After going to Pretoria as an avowed friend and adviser in the Boer cause, and failing to obtain the entire confidence of Paul Krüger and the other leaders, he went off on the other side. The book he published in the course of the war seems to afford documentary illustration of his double-sidedness. In a chapter dealing with the causes of the war, evidently written when he was hoping to be taken into the service of the Transvaal Government, after giving a good and, indeed, unanswerable statement of the Boer case, a final paragraph, apparently written just before going to press, is clumsily tacked on to what it is plain was originally intended to be the end of the chapter. This, while ignoring the whole of the previous argument, crudely sides with the aggressive Imperialist policy of Great Britain against the Dutch Republics. Farelly came over to England for a few weeks after the conclusion of peace, but I never met him again. He returned, after his brief sojourn in this country, to South Africa, where he shortly after died. Farelly was not without his good qualities, notably a certain Irish open-heartedness, but financial embarrassments apparently drove him, as they lave driven many others, into tortuous courses.

Before leaving the subject of my residence in the Temple, it may be interesting to mention that among the visitors to my chambers was the composer Leoncavallo, who one evening, shortly before the first performance of his *Pagliacci* at Covent Garden, came and played over on the piano for me the score of the new opera.

In 1897 I gave up my chambers in the Temple, having married a second time, after some years of widowerhood. My wife was the daughter of a Thuringian physician. The great political feature at the end of the nineties was the intrigues of the mining magnates of the Transvaal to bring about the conquest of the country by Great Britain in the interests of their financial oligarchy, which culminated in the outbreak of war in the Autumn of 1899. As is well-known, practically the whole of the Radical and Socialist elements in the country were on the side of the Boor Republics. The present writer did his share in the agitation of the ensuing years. We all felt at the time bitterly ashamed of our nationality, and were most of us furiously anti-patriotic, as British patriotism was then understood. I remember a group of us subscribed for a wreath to place on the bust of Kruger at the Paris Exhibition of 1900. The Dutch Consul in Paris, who I believe was a strong Tory and individualist, objecting to the declaration on the red ribbon of the wreath, to the effect that it was a tribute to the righteousness of the Boer cause in its resistance to the crime initiated by a gang of financial capitalists, had it removed. We appealed, however, to Dr. Leyds, who was then in Paris, and got it reinstated. Subsequent events, and notably the great times through which we have been passing lately, have obliterated to a considerable extent the memory of the South African War and the bitterness of feeling it engendered. It is well, however, for our national pride to recall the fact that it is not only the German people who can allow themselves by a little beating of the "jingo" patriotic drum to be made the tools of an infamous gang with influence in high places, in perpetrating or abetting a hideous and abominable crime. The scoundrels of Johannesburg and London who machined the South African War in 1899 are not intrinsically a whit better than the scoundrels in Berlin and Vienna who machined the European War of 1914. The difference is one of the magnitude in the issues of the crime, rather than in the intentions or acts of those guilty in bringing it about. It would be disastrous indeed if the result of the World War should be to increase the pompous self-righteousness of the British race and to blind the better part of the nation to the fact that profit-hungry capitalism, aggression, and militarism are intrinsically the same, and work the same evil results, in all peoples alike.

The end of the nineties and the opening of the twentieth century gave rise to the seemingly inevitable dispute as to the year from which the new century was to be reckoned as starting. The majority of the disputants were, if I remember rightly, in favour of 1901 as being the first year of the century, in spite of the fact of scientific authorities such as the late Lord Kevin opting for 1900. That this latter view is the only possibly correct one, I must confess, is to me so obvious that I can hardly conceive of any person of sense and education taking the opposite one. The century obviously begins with the first hour of the first year and not with the first hour of the second year. The cardinal number of the current year is plainly that of the last completed year. It is the ordinal number which gives you the real position of the yell in question. Thus a man on his fortieth birthday, let us say, is properly deemed to be just entering upon his forty-first year, and this notwithstanding the fact that he will continue to be reckoned forty years of age until his next birthday, i.e. the completion of his forty-first year, when, though "cardinally" forty-one, he will be "ordinally" in his forty-second year until his following birthday, and so on. A child when it is born enters upon the first year of its life. It does not begin its first year after it is one year old. The conclusion is obvious as regards the age of the so-called Christian Era itself. With the 1st of January 1900, by a parity of reasoning, it is clear that the Christian Era as a measure of time entered upon the 1901st year of its existence ; in other words, on the 1st of January 1900 the first year of the new century began, though of course it was not completed until the 1st of January 1901. It is indeed astonishing that this perfectly plain and obvious piece of arithmetic should not have been grasped by large numbers of persons, who were deceived by the cardinal number of the completed year 1 into regarding it as the ordinal or first year of the century. In this, as in so many other cases, the popular mind was deceived by a false analogy. It treated a measure of time having a beginning and ending as a concrete object in space irrespective of time. I have thought it worth while to devote a few remarks to this question, keenly debated as it was at the junction of the two centuries, inasmuch as, comparatively unimportant though it is, it aptly illustrates the stupidity of the average intelligence, and its inability accurately to gauge anything involving a little effort of thought discrimination. At the same time it shows its readiness to be led astray by a false analogy, provided it offers but the most superficial semblance of plausibility. It would scarcely be believed that this absurd controversy engendered so much heat at

152

the time that the matter came once or twice before the police courts in the form of assault cases, one gentleman having tried, or at least threatened, to throw his opponent on this burning question out at the door of the railway carriage in which they were sitting.

Altogether, the decade of the nineties had a character of its own, although not so strongly marked by new departures as that of the eighties. It continued, with certain modifications, the movements of the eighties, while adding little substantially to those movements. In its human element, the types entering upon manhood or womanhood during the nineties show little essential difference from those produced by the previous decade, beyond perhaps that increasing tendency to blaséness which was enshrined in the current phrase of the time – *fin de siècle*. The "decadence" of the life and point of view of the cultured middle-classes of the nineties was very pronounced, and was not confined, as was the "aestheticism" of the eighties, to a comparatively narrow circle of those who made a special pose of it. A general atmosphere of "decadence" seemed to pervade the intellectual middle-class circles of the decade in question, apart from conscious affectation. This, although it died down, or at least became modified, after the opening of the new century, nevertheless left its general mark upon English society, amid the rise of other movements and interests, until the outbreak of the World War in August 1914, and had a strong repercussion in new fashions in art, especially in painting and music. Bizarrerie and incoherence were the signs-manual of this movement.

# IX. The Mental Outlook of the England of To-Day and Yesterday

Writing as I now am, while the great European War is as yet unfinished, in speaking of the England of to-day I am perhaps hardly quite accurate. In due strictness I should have said the England of Midsummer 1914. But inasmuch as no new development has as yet arisen, the fact that the great wave of the war influences has for a moment submerged all other issues would hardly justify us in assuming that below this wave the ways of looking at things, at the period immediately preceding the war, do not still subsist, although for the moment obscured. That the years of the war will leave their profound mark on the British character, and especially on its attitude towards practical social and political issues, I regard as a certainty. But the change wrought by the war will probably mark its full measure some years after the conclusion of peace, and meanwhile the mental attitude, at least in theoretical matters, that obtained in the Summer of 1914 will maintain itself in essentials perhaps for a generation to come as the groundwork of the national world-view. I speak of "national world-view" as it is convenient and more germane to these reminiscences to regard these manifestations of modern thought as they express themselves in this country and as coloured by its habits and traditions, although of course, strictly speaking, there is nothing essential in modern types of thought that is purely provincial or national and not more or less common to the whole of civilized humanity, i.e. to all Europe and its colonies, including, of course, America, and not omitting Japan. But, as above said, it belongs to this work to deal more especially with the movements of thought of to-day and of the past generation as manifested in the English-speaking race, and especially in Great Britain itself. The temperament of the Anglo-Saxon race, moral and intellectual, has undoubtedly something peculiarly its own. This has become evident ever since the close of the Middle Ages, and it remained notably true till the end of the mid-Victorian period, as it is termed. Even now, notwithstanding the more cosmopolitan atmosphere of the last, and especially the current generation, it is a fact which has not lost its significance.

I have already dealt in earlier chapters with the rise and progress of the Socialist movement in Great Britain, and this, therefore, need not detain us here. What I propose to deal with in this chapter is the actual position of English popular thought – in short, of current opinion – towards certain religious, ethical, civic, and aesthetic questions as contrasted with two generations, and even one generation, ago.

First of all, let us examine the present position of the popular English mind towards certain problems usually regarded as at the basis of religious ideas. We have already seen how in the early sixties the crassest obscurantism, based on the current creed, prevailed in the moral and intellectual attitude of the whole middle class, and in fact with all but a few literary and specially intellectual circles. Things were just beginning to move then, but very slowly. Intellectual darkness and social terrorism, as described by the late Mr. Benn in his **History of English Rationalism during the nineteenth Century**, was but little shaken till quite the close of the sixties. The view that religion was necessary for the masses, and that anything tending to shake the belief or dull intellectual acquiescence of these same masses in the current theology was fraught with grievous danger to property and the State, and hence to be severely discountenanced, was commonly to be heard into the beginning of the seventies. That generation has now, however, passed away. The average man in society no longer thinks it necessary even to pretend to any belief in the dogmas of the Christian Churches, but it was long before the fundamental articles of theological belief ceased to be regarded as a necessary badge of respectability.[1] The question then arose how the problem was to be solved of not discarding the badge or social cachet while getting rid of the obligation to profess any positive belief in old Theistic dogma.

It was solved on the following lines. While it was felt that to avow Atheism under that name, or in any unequivocal form, would hive meant a serious rupture with the tradition of speculative respectability, a convenient way out was found by which a man with a social position to guard might retain his disbelief in Theism, while vehemently repudiating the charge of Atheism. A new word was coined to this end by the late Professor Huxley at one of the gatherings of the old Metaphysical Society, which used to meet in the early eighties at the late Mr. James Knowles' house on Clapham Common. To save his social and speculative respectability, the Atheist had now only to call himself an Agnostic and he was comparatively all right. A somewhat doubtful line of distinction was sought to be drawn between the alleged point of view of the despised and rejected Atheist and the relatively acceptable Agnostic. The Atheist, it was said, was a foolish, if not wicked person, who thought he could prove the non-existence of God. The Agnostic, on the other hand, was, whether one agreed with him or not, a decent and reasonable person, who did not deny the Theistic contention, but merely asserted the necessary absence of all proof of that contention as being deducible from the nature of human knowledge. The absence of any categorical denial on his part thus saved the situation as regards respectability for the happy Agnostic.

Now, as to the alleged ground of distinction between the scorned and the tolerated opinion, if we examine it, we shall find, I think, that it is more vulnerable to criticism than its protagonists imagined. In the first place it may fairly be doubted whether the Atheist supposed ever existed in the flesh – in short, whether he is not a dummy man of straw, set up by the Agnostic for the purpose of being knocked down again. Personally, I cannot recall the case of any reputed Atheist who claimed that he could prove the non-existence of the Deity as a general proposition, although he may have contended that some particular conception or definition of such a Being involved inconsistencies or even

157

absurdities. It is certain, however, that before the days of Agnosticism any one who repudiated a positive belief in the Theists' dogma, on the ground that the evidence of its truth was lacking, would have been counted an Atheist. But in the second place, even admitting the theoretical validity of the distinction sought to be drawn by the Agnostic between his own position and that of the Atheist, it is not difficult to show that it has no practical importance, or even significance, whatever. Between the absence of all proof of an affirmative and the presence of the proof of a negative there may be a logical distinction, but it is without practical results. We see this even in ordinary life, in a weaker form, in the distinction between an impossibility and a high degree of improbability.

Here, also, the undoubtedly sound theoretical distinction has no bearing whatever on conduct. I take an illustration I have given elsewhere. The ordinary suburban resident believes in the possibility of the fall of aerolites, and he disbelieves in basilisks (let us say); in other words, he regards the latter as an absurdity, or an impossibility. Nevertheless, if he is contemplating an evening stroll on Clapham Common, he will be just as little concerned with the undoubted possibility, albeit high improbability, of having his head smashed by the fall of an aerolite, as he would be with the absurdity or impossibility of his being scorched by the glance of a basilisk. For practical purposes there is thus no distinction between theoretical impossibility and theoretical possibility, when the probability falls below a certain standard. Hence, to come back to our original point, the Atheist's alleged belief that the non-existence of a deity can be demonstrated, and the Agnostic's admitted conviction that the nature of human knowledge precludes the possibility of any positive demonstration, or even probable proof, of his existence, amounts for practical purposes to precisely the same thing. Yet if the distinction commonly alleged between the Atheist and the Agnostic rests on what is little better than a logical quibble, it is not impossible perhaps, if we try, to discover a real distinction.

But should we do so, it is in the region of ethical sentiment, rather than logic or speculative theory, that we must look for it.

While conceding the impossibility of proving the negative of the Theist's contention, the Atheist may be supposed to address the Theist as follows:

"Even admitting the truth of your speculative position as to the existence of some sort of personality who is the creator and orderer of the Universe, there is nothing in the nature of the ordering of this Universe that would entitle me to regard such a being as an object worthy of my worship. To any argument based on the imperfections or positive evils of which the ordering of the world is full, you Theists of all sects and persuasions content yourselves with replying by vague assurances that, to use a vulgar metaphor, 'it will all come out in the washing' – that all is meant for the best, and will ultimately turn out to be for the best. In fact, in your theology and ethics you accept the position of the victim of the confidence-trick man. Just as the former is willing to hand over his cash into the keeping of a person of whose *bona fides* he has no evidence, so you are prepared to pledge your faith and religious ideal on the unproven assumption that the author and providence of this Universe is ethically good, and that all is for the best in this best of all possible worlds. Now, I am not prepared to do this. Nay, further, I find you are acting more foolishly even than the victim of the confidence-trick man. The latter is usually a plausible person, at least, and his victim has nothing definite on which to base his suspicions. The case with the creator and providence whose existence you assume is far otherwise. Here the horrors and evils present in the world of his supposed creation and ordering are very real, and obtrude themselves upon our notice. In the face of these facts my conscience will not allow me to regard the

159

author or permitter (for that matter) of these things as worthy of my respect, not to say adoration. I am not to be beguiled by cheap references to the limitations of the human faculty, by tall talk about 'wise purposes,' 'beneficent ends,' etc., in excuse for the ways of your assumed deity.

"The limitations of the human viewpoint cannot possibly justify us without other adequate grounds in concluding the very opposite of what that viewpoint indicates. The distinction sought to be drawn between action and permission, to palliate from the Theistic point of view the evils of the world, is futile. If I permit a wrong to be perpetrated which I could prevent, I am at least passively guilty of that wrong. To plead it as an excuse would be, in fact, a mean attempt to evade the moral judgment that condemns me. There is a well-known legal maxim which says '*qui facit per alium facit per se.*' There are, moreover, certain actions and omissions, certain vile and mean lines of conduct, which no end can justify as means. The most pious bourgeois condemns the conduct of the little boy who steals-money from the till in order to put it in the missionary-box, or of the gambler who cheats at cards in order to maintain his aged mother, yet conduct which he would reprove in the little boy or the cardsharper he condones in his God. That the end justifies the means may possibly in some cases be admitted as regards Man, with his limited outlook and powers of action. But I submit that on any ethical basis it can never apply as an excuse for the *prima facie* evil acts of a being possessed of the power and knowledge assumed in the notion of God as the creator and providence of this world. For my conscience no amount of 'wise purposes' or 'beneficent ends' will exonerate the author of the world as it is. They are to me as the 'good intentions' with which the way to Hell is said to be paved.

The transparent sophistry of theologians in attempting the impossible task of justifying their divinity fills me with nothing but disgust and loathing."


Thus the Atheist. This moral attitude might possibly be regarded as differentiating the conscientious Atheist from the mere Agnostic. According to this definition, the Atheist is essentially ethical and religious in his judgment, while the Agnostic need not be so. It must be admitted, however, that the Atheist thus becomes an anti-Theist.[2]

One of the most striking phenomena of social change in the present generation, the counterpart of the rise and domination of Imperialism in politics, is the installation of imperialistic or patriotic sentiment in the place of the old religious feeling. Patriotism, as it is called, has undoubtedly taken the place formerly occupied by Christian sentiment and aspiration in the mind of the average man. This was noticeable enough before the war, but the war, of course, has thrown it into the strongest possible relief. In how many thousands of those who have volunteered for the front do we not find the ideal object for which they are prepared to sacrifice themselves to be England or the British Empire. And yet how many of those who profess, and sincerely profess, attachment to England as their ideal object, if they thought a little, would not have to admit that there is much in England, politically, socially, and morally, of which they disapprove! Yet this does not prevent the ideal of nationality from dominating their whole emotional being. Of course, to a great extent the present-day religion of patriotism has been worked up more or less artificially in the Press and on the political platform. The new religion of Patriotism is even preached by the different Christian sects as the modern expression of their creed. It is inculcated through the Boy Scouts' movement and in the present-clay education of our youth. For the religion of Patriotism, the national or imperial State is the *ultima ratio*. It does not recognize any organism or collectivity as object of conduct higher than the

State. Hurnanitv is for it a mere phrase. The solidarity, moreover, of those scattered through many existing States, holding like views and like aspirations, never suggests itself to it as perhaps an intrinsically higher object of conduct than any existing State, on the analogy of the mediaeval conception of Christendom. The only alternative to this erection of imperialistic jingo sentiment, under the name of Patriotism, into a religion, is Socialism. The aspiration towards a classless society and international brotherhood is for Socialism a supreme ideal of life and conduct.

The whole outlook of to-day shows the complete loss of hold of the older faith on modern society. The change of mental attitude between now and fifty years ago is enormous. It would perhaps not be going too far to say that the difference between the mental outlook of the average man of 1866 and of 1916 is quite as great as, if not greater than, that between the man of 1866 and the corresponding man of 1766. Such has been the acceleration of the tempo of social and intellectual changes within the last two generations.

Amid the various movements indicating modified views of the relations of life, what is known as the woman's movement has not failed to attract much attention. I do not propose here to discuss this question at any length. I have already done so elsewhere.[3] But there are certain of its aspects with which one is continually confronted at the present day. The freeing of women from the conventional bonds of the society of fifty years ago has had a wide influence: among other things, it has had the result of producing a new set of sex-illusions in men. The scorning and disparagement of the old idea of the domestic function as being pre-eminently the raison *d'être* of woman, which has become the commonplace of many advanced circles, has led, on the one hand, to the illusion among men that they must look in their womankind not merely for sexual fidelity, and kindliness in word and conduct, but for intellectual companionship, and to the reading into their relations with their wives and other female associates an intellectual companionship which is not there. On the other hand, it has led in women to the cultivation of self-assertion and priggery, in order to make up in the eyes of men for their real intellectual deficiencies. The assumption of intellectual independence gives to the woman of the present day a special impress. Yet it is noteworthy that after the complete social and intellectual emancipation of the female sex, which has been going on now for well-nigh two generations (reckoning from its first beginnings), that the number of really eminent women of the first class has not increased. The George Sands, George Eliots, the Rosa Bonheurs, the Charlotte Brontes, all belong to the period when women were not emancipated as they are now. What has the present day to show on the score of female geniuses? That there are a sufficiency of intelligent and able women going about is of course not to be denied, but I can only recall one who could be quoted as showing an intellectual calibre which could take its place in that of the front rank of men in the same department. In the authoress of **Themis** we undoubtedly have, even more than in the women of earlier generations mentioned above, an intellectual power and flexibility of intellect which may truly be termed masculine.

Otto Weininger, in his book **Sex and character**, remarks upon the fact that in both the sexes you usually find a more or less of ingredient of the opposite sex. This may be slight and almost inappreciable, or it may be an important factor. It may manifest itself also in various ways, physically, morally, and intellectually, but the appearance at rare intervals of a woman with an exceptional muscular development, an exceptional strength of purpose (a Lady Macbeth, a Joanne d'Arc, etc.) or of intellectual perception, approaching or equalling that of the first rank of men in the same department, may fairly be regarded as examples of *lusus naturae,* rather than as indicating any general potentialities on the part of the female sex. Had there been anything approaching real equality in mental disposition between the sexes, this equality should, I contend, have shown itself in the course of the last half century in an unmistakable manner, and this it certainly has not done.

Those who are forever contending for the average intellectual equality of women with men, it is difficult to believe do so in complete *bona fides*. They studiedly ignore that prominent characteristic of the human female, the inability to follow out a logical argument, coupled with the unwillingness to admit the plainest fact or proof which tells against a cherished prejudice or emotion. How often do we find a woman, confronted by such fact or proof, stop her ears, or rush out of the room with some such phrase as "Oh, leave off, I can't bear it!" I would ask the apostles of female equality if they have ever heard of a man acting in this way. Or, again, how many women they have known who do not change their opinions with their moods, or with changes in their relations with persons. The sort of conduct referred to belongs to the hysterical side of woman, of which so many aspects present themselves to common observation, but which Feminist advocates are often found dishonest enough to ignore or even to deny.

With all the talk of equality between the sexes, we find the notion of chivalry, based upon the opposite theory of woman's physical and mental weakness, "moult no feather." Women, as before remarked, are to have all the rights and responsibilities of men so long as these are honourable and agreeable, but there is no serious suggestion amongst Feminists that they should give up any of the privileges "chivalry" (so called) accords them by virtue of their sex. Evidence galore of this is to be found, not only in the comparatively unimportant manners and customs of everyday life, but in our courts of law, criminal and civil. We never hear a hint from the side of the woman's movement that men and women convicted respectively of the same, equally heinous, offences should have the same measure of punishment meted out to them. There is no notion among the Feminist fraternity that what is sauce for the gander should also be sauce for the goose. On the contrary, every effort is made by the pretended advocates of equality to emphasize and strengthen the so-called chivalric sentiment, based on an entirely different view of the respective powers and capacities of the sexes, together with the consequences as regards female privilege deducible from that sentiment.[4] Such, in a few words, describes the body of opinion known as the woman's movement up to the early Summer of 1914.

The attitude of public opinion as regards the marriage question, though partly coloured by the view taken of the woman question generally, is by no means altogether so. On the contrary, it runs frequently on independent lines. The question of the right of the State to determine the private relations of the individual in the matter of sex is one which has acquired increasing prominence during the present generation. Although long before the matter of private reflexion and discussion among the thoughtful, it was lifted into the arena of public debate largely through the publication by the late Mr. Grant Allen of his didactic novel, **The Woman Who Did**. Viewed on rationalistic principles, and apart from theological prepossessions or ethical prejudices deriving or surviving from earlier social conditions, it has become to many persons increasingly doubtful whether the sex relation in itself is a subject belonging to morality at all, any more than the exercise of any other physiological function. This, of course, at first sight wears the aspect of an astounding paradox. But it may be observed that I italicize the words *in itself*. For it is quite clear that in the general run of human conduct it often involves, owing to the conditions surrounding it, serious moral considerations. But the distinction between this sex question considered *per se* and *per aliud* has never as yet been kept sufficiently in view. Granting the distinction named, the question resolves itself into how far society is justified by moral pressure, or still more, through its organ the State, by compulsory legal enactment, in interfering with what is *au fond* a purely private and personal question for the individual man or woman. The chief point, of course, in which the sex-relation of the individual affects society in general, in fact, we may say the only

165

point in which it directly affects it, is the question of offspring. How far can the welfare of offspring be effectively safeguarded in society as at present constituted? Is the coercion of the individual, either by moral pressure or by legal compulsion, such as the existing Marriage Laws, necessary, or is it the most effective way of achieving the end in view? An increasing body of opinion among the thinking classes of the community is tending to pronounce against the necessity and even against the practical expediency of the existing coercive Marriage Laws, and in favour of the constituting of the marriage relation as an entirely free union, or at best as one in which the law would only concern itself, as in other cases of contract, with the enforcement of the conditions, if any, originally agreed upon between the parties themselves. Marriage would become thenceforth another case of the oft-quoted principle enunciated by the late Sir Henry Maine, that legal progress is from status to contract. It is certainly difficult to see that the retention of the marriage relation as a status has been productive of the happiness or well-being of the community. That other and more efficient means of safeguarding the welfare of children than such as aim at the legal handcuffing together of the parents and the hampering of their personal freedom – for this is the result of the Marriage Laws of to-day – will hardly admit of a doubt by any open-minded person who has given the subject his careful consideration. The progress made within the last few years in intelligent public opinion as regards this question is indeed remarkable. The question of marriage has at least reached the stage in which opinions differing from the traditional and conventional ones are admitted as being reasonably and honestly held, and acted upon, by many people. It is noteworthy that some of the Suffragette leaders profess to be champions of the conventional opinions in the matter in question. Is this with a view to winning over reactionary opinion, or is it for the purpose of maintaining the unfair incidence of the present coercive Marriage Laws upon the husband, whereby the wife is enabled to browbeat him at her pleasure. In any case, the question of free or legal marriage union can at most be one of civil expediency rather than of morals. The subjecting oneself or not to a legal form, whichever way it be decided, cannot possibly be a question of morality or immorality.

Leaving social and political matters and reverting to those of religious or speculative interest, a word should be said on the comparative success in the early nineties of that singular personality known as Madame Blavatsky. Whether impostor, as most people regarded her, or not, she certainly had a somewhat sensational success in the declining years of the last century. The speculative tenets she promulgated, under the name Theosophy, or, as I believe it was originally termed, Esoteric Buddhism, were, as Professor Rhys Davies assured me, when they received their first boom, not Buddhist at all, but represented the common Yogi doctrines of India. As a matter of fact, we may trace them in Europe at least as long ago as the second century with its Gnostic systems. Especially may be noticed in this connexion the writing known as the **Pistis Sophia**. But mystic doctrines of a similar character are traceable in various parts of Southern and Western Asia long before the Christian Era, and, as we all know, spread throughout the Roman Empire with considerable success during the first and second centuries. They seem to have a tendency to reappear whenever a particular civilization becomes worn out and its traditional shibboleths and the notions previously binding it together are rapidly going into the melting-pot. It is true that, in our present transitional period, the ideal of social evolution has fur the first time appeared above the horizon of human thought and aspiration in a definite form, but it is not yet strong enough to supersede the old interest, among the thoughtful, in the fortunes of the individual personality or soul. To overcome, even in thought, this self-centredness of the individual self-consciousness and its interests, in favour of that which from its own standpoint is external to, and apparently detached from, itself, is indeed a hard thing for most men. Such an attitude may indeed, as every great crisis shows, obtain sporadically on a wave of exceptional enthusiasm, and be the stimulus to the most heroic self-sacrifice,

167

but it does not endure as a permanent state of mind. Jaurès puts the thing trenchantly (**L'Armée Nouvelle**, p.404). Speaking with reference to the hopelessness of countless individual lives and destinies under Capitalism: *"Quand on songe que dans notre univers encore barbare, la vie et la conscience sont discontinues; que chaque centre de sensibilité est impénétrable aux autres; que pour l'individu la douleur individuelle est un absolu; que la continuité et infinité des choses sont encore tout exterieures et superficielles; que pour tout être vivant la loi se résume tout entière en son propre destin; que la trame illimitée du temps est déchirée en autant de lambeaux qu'il y a d'êtres éphémères, et que, par un surcroit de dureté et de scandale, beaucoup ont souffert et meurent sans avoir meme entrevu a quoi leur douleur et leur mort peuvent servir; quand on pense en effet a tout cela, il n'y a pas de progres social qui puisse pleinement consoler de toutes les souffrances qui en furent la rançon."*

It is undoubtedly the feeling to which Jaurès refers in this passage, of the absoluteness and intranslatability, so to say, of the individual personality and its interests, which is the stumbling-block with many in the way of an ideal, for which any given personality is rather accidental than essential. And the strength of this feeling still remaining it is on which theories of the supernatural, including many a new quackery, base their success in the modern world. This was undoubtedly the soil in which Madame Blavatsky's propaganda struck root. The rejection of Christian dogma does not necessarily mean any lack of interest on the part of the individual in the destiny and fortunes of his own soul. The dogmatic assurances of Christian Theology in this connexion having lost their hold, refuge is sought in other means of consolement. Although I would not for a moment be understood as placing the two movements on the same level, the above remarks apply, as already- observed, at least to some extent, to the Psychical Research Society. The latter, there is no doubt, represents a movement based on scientific lines and run by men of scientific standing. But the motive inspiring many of those who take an interest in it may unquestionably be found in the clinging of many minds to the individual soul and its fortunes. It would be futile to deny the existence of this feeling in some of the best of us, but it is also absurd to pretend that, natural though it may be, there is anything specially high and noble in it, and that, on the contrary, those who find their strongest concern and supremest aspiration in the realization of a higher humanity do not represent a loftier ideal than the seekers after the destiny of their own souls.

We may conclude this chapter by noticing, in contrast to modern notions, one or two specimens of the bourgeois wisdom of one's youth which have long since lost their savour. They afford an insight into the mentality of the British middle-class man of the early- and mid-Victorian epoch. These pieces of wisdom were coined for the purpose of edification. Thus, the youth of that period were seriously told, as an argument against the use of strong language, that it was undignified, since it implied that the man who swore did not consider his own bare word as carrying enough weight of itself to guarantee the truth of what he said. The idea of any one taking this somewhat wire-drawn piece of casuistry seriously seems funny at the present day. It would be interesting to know whether many ingenuous youths of, say, the fifties and sixties of the last century were really deterred from the expression of their feelings "in well set terms" by the terrible implication that their doing so meant that they undervalued their own character for veracity. The habitual use of strong language on any and every occasion, we may agree, is to be deprecated, as both indicating and tending to encourage an unbalanced emotional temper. But there is no doubt that there are occasions on which the employment of purpled speech is not only a useful and salutary vent to the feelings, but also impresses the hearer. In any case, the reason for abstaining from it excogitated by the pious Victorian brain is characteristic and amusing, if not convincing.

Another select specimen of edificatory Victorian wisdom

on somewhat similar lines to the last may be found in the appraisement of the moral bearings of suicide, which consisted in the assertion that the man who took his own life exhibited cowardice in so doing, since his act was a proof that he lacked the courage to face the responsibilities of existence. Now, we may fairly ask ourselves whether the good Victorian souls, who felt it their duty to put forward this thesis for the sake of edification, did not do so with their tongues in their cheeks. The unsophisticated human being knows that the man who deliberately faces death in any form, and whether self-inflicted or not, is the very opposite of a coward. He may be everything else that you like, but he is most assuredly not a coward. The willingness to face death, no matter for what cause, whether it be good or bad, is of itself an all-convincing guarantee at least of one virtue – courage. No amount of feeble paradoxical casuistry will suffice to stamp the man who is prepared to do this, whatever be his motives, as other than a brave man. The universally accepted definitions of courage and cowardice essentially involve this, and the *bona fides* of the goody-goody Victorian moralist who would have called it in question his sophistications may fairly be doubted. We know, of course, that the habit of tampering with truth for the sake of edification is not a new one, but its ethical justification is, to put it mildly, at least highly debatable.

One of the gems of the *bourgeois* wisdom of the Victorian era, which was supposed by its votaries to be crushing as against all theories of economic equality, was the assumption that poverty was the result of laziness, and wealth of industry on the part of its possessors. According to the assumption in question, the existence side by side in the same society of a working class and a capitalist class was due to the fact that one set of human beings, or its progenitors, was idle and thriftless, and another set industrious and thrifty. The working classes, the wage-earners, those who live by the toil of their hands, represented the first class, those who possessed wealth and lived on their incomes-in a word, the aristocracy and the middle classes-stood for the second.

The exact way in which this great economic difference came about was never explained; but the worthy *bourgeois* none the less persuaded himself, or professed to have persuaded himself, into a belief that it was even so – that once upon a time there existed a lot of idle, worthless rascals side by side with another set of frugal and industrious saints, and that these two sets of persons were the progenitors and the protagonists of the poor and the rich classes of to-day respectively, to whose descendants the vices of the one class the virtues and of the other had been for the most part transmitted. The above is no exaggeration of the social and economic beliefs of otherwise fairly well-educated people in this country a generation or two ago. That, speaking generally, poverty- has no more to do with idleness and thriftlessness, or wealth with industry and frugality, thorn either have with the spots on the sari, is a proposition the average bourgeois mind of the England of the fifties and the sixties of the last century would have confessed itself altogether unable to grasp. The sociological views of our grandparents on this question afford another illustration of the often-noted fact that, if the sheerest nonsense be only enough repeated and dinned into the ears of people by themselves and others, it will be accepted without further investigation as though it were a proved scientific fact. Of course, in this case the acceptance of the doctrine in question was aided by the class interest, which led to the wish to believe what was pleasant and consoling to itself.

The above illustrations are, I think, fair specimens of the lines on which the popular middle-class wisdom of a couple of generations ago ran. The idea was always edification – edification, that is, from the current *bourgeois* point of view – first, truth and correct reasoning very much afterwards.

We may remark, by the way, that we find substantially the same thing to-day in what is known as "judge-made law," especially criminal law. All such judicial decisions will be found on examination to have for their end, not the logical interpretation of a law or statute, but "edification" from the judge's point of view, to wit, the enlarging of the scope of the law as much as feasible, i.e. the bringing as many acts as possible under its ban. Thus, the decision by which, in the case of two persons agreeing to commit suicide together, and only one of them dying, the survivor is chargeable with the murder of his partner; or that other decision, according to which any one unintentionally causing the death of another person, through the perpetration of an illegal act, is likewise guilty of the crime of wilful murder, are both plainly at variance with justice, as they are with any reasonable or common-sense definition of the crime of wilful murder. These decisions, especially the last named, even amount to an impudent violation of the obvious intention of the common law, the element of wilfulness being plainly absent. It is the same with most other cases of decision-law. Statutes are wrenched out of their sockets, with the aid of the most transparent casuistry, to make them cover cases they were never meant to cover, to satisfy the lust of the judiciary for the manufacture of new crimes or the enhancing of the severity of punishment in the case of old ones, thereby increasing their own power over their victims. The flagrant and shameless violation of principle, of logic, and of right judgment in the interpretation of law by the judiciary in the interests of this theory, that it is desirable to catch as many victims a; possible in the net of the law, and thereby augment the power of its administrators, amounts to a scandal.

What changes the great World War will make in the general character of the British mind in its activities and receptivities it is of course impossible to say as yet, but, as already pointed out in the beginning of the present chapter, it seems hardly likely that views and ways of looking at things will undergo an immediate and complete transformation, although they can hardly fail to be modified by the crisis through which the world has passed since the Summer of 1914. Meanwhile, I offer these admittedly detached remarks on certain aspects of the nineteenth and early twentieth century thought to be followed up at will by those interested.

## Notes

1. Even to-day we see the remains of the old obscurantist sentiment flickering in certain quarters. Thus, in journals and publications intended for general reading, we commonly find a tendency to defend as much of whilom orthodox opinion as is possible in the face of modern knowledge and modern thought generally. In any doubtful point the case is mostly presented to the general reader with the scales weighted in favour of the less heterodox view, whatever that may be. This may be regarded, let us hope, as a last dying rumble of the old intolerant thunder.

2. I have often thought that, given a new Dante or Milton, a great epic might be written on Theistic lines, entitled The Remorse of God, understanding by God a personal or quasi-personal creator and providence. The idea would be, admitting the essential moral goodness of the latter, his gradual awakening to a sense of the moral perversion and wickedness involved in the doing or permitting of evil for the problematical achievement of "wise purposes" and "beneficent ends."

3. E.g. in the Fraud of Feminism (Grant Richards).

4. A striking illustration of the unfair twist to emotion given by the chivalric sentiment was afforded during the present war by the Cavell case. Amid all the admiration showered upon Edith Cavell, and indignation at her execution, not one word was heard of the case of the Belgian architect, Philippe Bancq, who was shot for precisely the same offence, at the same time and place, as Edith Cavell herself!

# X. Variorum Reminiscences and Reflexions

It may not be amiss to say a few words on some of the more noteworthy men I have known otherwise than in connexion with the Socialist movement. Let us begin with Philosophy. Foremost amongst the Englishmen who took an active part in what was known as the "Young" or Neo-Hegelian movement in this country was Richard Burdon Haldane (now Lord Haldane), I first met Haldane in 1882, when this movement in Philosophy was at its height, having driven back the old English empirical or associational school (to employ a military metaphor) to its second and third line of defences. In a word, the British empirical school, whose doctrines had long been thought the final word in Philosophy, was already regarded by the up-to-date men as old-fashioned and commonplace. I saw Haldane for the first time at a meeting of the old Aristotelian Society, at which he spoke in favour of the Neo-Hegelian position. Our acquaintance ripened, and he used sometimes to come down to Croydon, where I was then living, on a Sunday, and many a walk I have had with him on the Surrey hills. Among the smaller incidents of these walks I remember, while we were crossing a field, Haldane's impressing upon me the legal point that should any question of trespass arise in such a case, the correct thing was to tender a small coin for technical damage to the owner or his agent, with the words "I claim no right," which should stop all further proceedings.

I can well recall a Sunday in 1885 when he arrived and informed me that he was about to devote himself to a political career, and had entered as Liberal candidate for Haddingtonshire. He proceeded to argue that the principles of Gladstonian Liberalism represented the political outcome or reflex of the Hegelian thought-movement of the "*Idée*." A discussion ensued, in which I traversed his main position alike in Philosophy and in politics. Later on the champion of Woman Suffrage Bills,

175

Haldane at this time and for some years after was opposed to the movement, remarking to me on one occasion that the main object many of these women had in desiring the suffrage was to force rascally and unjust laws against men onto the Statute-book. It is to be regretted, from the point of view of consistency, that Haldane subsequently undertook the ministerial piloting through the House of Lords of that most infamous piece of anti-male legislation, the so-called "White Slavery Act" of 1912.

Throughout his career Haldane has never abandoned his devotion to Hegel, and always has a portrait of the great German thinker near him in the room where he is working. This, together with his well-known appreciation of German thought and German literature generally, has undoubtedly been the cause of some of the attacks with which he has been assailed, with insinuations as to his being a "pro-German," during the present war. Whatever view we may take of Haldane's career as a politician, or of his theoretical opinions, political or otherwise, there is no doubt that he has been subjected to most unfair criticism, which is really based on the fact of his interest in the intellectual side of German life. As regards another of the accusations against him, we must never forget that a man who has not the point of view of Socialist criticism as regards all existing Capitalist governments, and hence who does not distrust them *ab initio*, is very likely, with the best intentions, to be befouled in his diplomatic intercourse. Besides, even apart from this, a thinker is not necessarily the best judge of character or a good reader of the intentions of men, and I for one can see nothing remarkable in the fact that Haldane, in the Spring of 1912, acting in perfect good faith, allowed himself to be, partly at least, beguiled by the Kaiser and the clever and unscrupulous politicians of the Wilhelmstrasse. After all, Haldane's real interests have always lain in Philosophy. The real Haldane is Haldane the metaphysician. Haldane the politician is merely the ordinary, intriguing manipulator of one of the traditional parties in the State.

Of the rest of my philosophical friends and acquaintances, with the exception of Eduard von Hartmann, already referred to on a previous page, I can recall no name that would interest the general reader save that of Henri Bergson. I met Bergson for the first time at a dinner given in his honour by Mr. Wildon Carr at the Savile Club, when he was in England some few years ago. This dinner was an interesting one from many points of view. We all made afterdinner speeches I remember – Shaw, Zangwill, Graham Wallas, myself, and others, besides the guest of the evening, all contributing their quota. As may be expected, the "*élan vital*" and the "*durée*" figured largely in many of these discourses. Bergson, as he told me afterwards, was much gratified with the evening's entertainment, and with the sociableness and informality that characterized the proceedings. I subsequently saw Bergson on different occasions in Paris, and had some interesting conversations with him. On my questioning Bergson as to why he had not dealt with certain of what are usually- regarded as the fundamental problems of Metaphysics, he replied that as yet he had not done so, as he had had his special work to do, which was to emphasize Reality as an interpenetrative movement of which Time was the essential element, in opposition to the older Metaphysics, for which the arrested moment of consciousness, reproduced in reflexion, on the analogy of spacial relation, was regarded as the *prius* of the world of living reality. He said further that he doubted whether the time was ripe as yet for a complete philosophic synthesis. The evolution of philosophic thought, he was of opinion, should follow a course similar to the evolution of physical science. Each worker in the field of Philosophy should, like the scientific investigator, work at his own special problem as far as possible, without attempting to spread himself over the whole field and reduce all problems equally under his purview. The time would then eventually come, each separate problem being thoroughly worked out, for the elaboration of a complete and systematic philosophic synthesis.

Bergson has told me that he was a contemporary of Jaurès as an undergraduate at the University of Paris, and, if I remember rightly, also of Sorel, the well-known writer on Syndicalism and Anarchism. Speaking of the feminist question, he expressed himself as opposed to female suffrage at the present time, but as regards the question of comparative intellectual power as between the sexes, he stated that, in looking over the exercises of his pupils, he was often unable to pronounce upon the sex of the writer until he saw the signature at the end. Respecting this point, however, I may recall to mind the remark made to me by Professor Sinzheimer, of Munich, as the result of his observation, to the effect that while in the first year or two of their university career he found that female students, as a rule, showed little or no inferiority in their work to men, yet that after this they rapidly "tailed off," and that at the conclusion of their course of studies, the difference between the male and female students who were contemporaries, i.e. who had entered the university at the same time, was often very considerable indeed. To return to Bergson. He is one of the marvels of the age, not so much on account of his undoubted genius and literary gift of presenting the special philosophic problem or problems with which he concerns himself, as for his power of attracting the extra-philosophic popular mind. Bergson's reputation outside the philosophic world, properly so-called, is not only greater than that of any other contemporary thinker, but there are probably few metaphysicians in the past who have enjoyed a popular fame while living anything like equal to that of the amiable and brilliant professor at the Collège de France.

Of my friend Boulting, whose excellent work on Giordano Bruno has lately been published, I have already spoken on an earlier page. Hitherto the only writings of his before the public have related to Italian history.

The International Congresses of Philosophy, to the institution of which Mr. Wildon Carr, who retired from the City to give his whole time to the interests of Philosophy, has devoted himself, were abruptly interrupted by the outbreak of the European War, just when arrangements had been made for holding the fifth Congress in London in 1915. Of the usefulness of such gatherings in the furtherance of investigation and discussion of the leading problems in the various departments of Philosophy there can be no question.

While on the subject of Philosophy, I cannot refrain from protesting against a practice dear to many academic exponents of the subject. It is a practice which may, I suppose, in the modern world be regarded as dating from Spinoza. I refer to the habit of giving to the Absolute the appellation God. This seems to me to be utterly unjustifiable from every point of view. The temptation to court popularity by using a popular theological term, nevertheless, seems to be irresistible to some thinkers. But it is a fraud and a deception, notwithstanding. The Absolute of which the philosopher speaks is not only not identical with God as ordinarily understood, but has hardly any analogy therewith. Not only the man in the street, but all persons, educated or uneducated, outside the special ranks of philosophical students, know roughly what they mean by God, and this meaning is not that of the Absolute of the metaphysician. The word God, outside Spinoza and later thinkers who have followed him, has always had a theological connotation. It has always stood for a personal or quasi-personal Being over against the world, who has created and who orders the world, as a despot orders his government, or, if you prefer it, as a loving father of patriarchal days ordered his household. Now, the Absolute of Philosophy has nothing whatever to do with this. By the Absolute is meant simply the ultimate principle which the analysis of conscious experience discloses as its own ultimate ground. It lies altogether outside the Theistic assumption. And it is, I submit, a gross deception to attempt by juggling with a word to befool the man who is seeking what Professor Gilbert Murray terms the "friend behind phenomena," with something totally different. I know that many intrinsically honest thinkers have been guilty of this subterfuge

179

(as it seems to me). Even such a straightforward man as the late Jean Jaurès, in his otherwise excellent and acute treatise, **De la realité du monde sensible,** has not been above resorting to it, a circumstance, by the way, which necessitated an explanation on his part when challenged as to his real meaning on one occasion in the French Chamber. Verily, Spinoza's **Deus sine natura** has much to answer for! The example of the great Jewish philosopher has been only too largely followed by a host of *epigoni* up to the present day. To my thinking, as above said, to cheat the unfortunate creature hankering after the "friend behind phenomena" with the Absolute of Metaphysics is grossly unfair. What he wants is a personality over against himself, and not a metaphysical postulate embracing himself, no matter how "spiritual" the terms in which it may be interpreted.

For the rest, the increasing interest in the higher issues of speculative thought, even though its growth may be slow, is nevertheless an undoubted fact and an encouraging one. The number of people, outside purely academic circles, who take an interest in these problems is unquestionably greater than ever before. This is, of course, partly one side merely of the general spread of intellectual activity and intellectual interests among ever widening sections of the population. There is perhaps, as a consequence of the above, too much tendency to regard Philosophy as no more than a branch of general literature. But while duly discounting this fact, we are justified, I think, nevertheless, in concluding that there is far greater genuine interest and intellectual alertness, with the average intelligent man of to-day, as regards these subjects, than was the case with a similar man of (say) a couple of generations ago. At that time, the theological interest was uppermost with the serious-minded. To-day, the metaphysical interest has at least partially entered into its inheritance, the major part of human interest being necessarily and justly occupied by the problems of the physical sciences, and still more of the human sciences.

The popularity of Bergson, though partly literary and

partly mere fashion, nevertheless helps to confirm the above remarks. The British interest in Kant or Hegel, or, so far as France is concerned, in Victor Cousin, was in its day not a tithe of that shown to-day in the case of Bergson. One thing is also of prime importance, and that is the general consensus of conviction that no subject of human knowledge can be treated adequately in an isolated manner, but that, in the last resort, all derive from the subject-matter of the problems with which Philosophy deals. The old theory that metaphysics is vanity has given way before a sense of the fact that the problems raised by metaphysics cannot be finally ignored or explained away, but that the human mind is doomed to seek some solution of them; if not a final solution, at least one which shall satisfy it for the present, while awaiting the more adequate one that time must inevitably bring with it. As to whether a final, in the sense of a fully adequate, solution will ever be reached, is a question the discussion of which would lie outside a book of reminiscences and more or less cursory reflexions.

Reverting from this digression into the regions of the "higher thought" to the reminiscence side of my present labours, the late poet, William Sharp, I may take as a specimen of the purely literary man. Sharp had no real interests outside pure literature. He had no special convictions on political or social matters, or on speculative questions, save insofar as they presented themselves in the guise of literary form and style. During the years 1879-80 I saw a good deal of Sharp and had many walks with him. I invariably found that all other interests with him were superficial, and contributory to the "stylistic" interest which was always the dominant one. His ambitions were purely literary, and one felt in his case what Morris used to say of Swinburne, that he ought to have been born between two calf covers. My general impression of Sharp was that while his literary faculty was obvious, he was an inconstant, uncertain, and whimsical person, liable to moods and affectations of moods, that often made themselves apparent alike socially and in his literary efforts. If I am not mistaken, Shaw, on more than one occasion, in reviewing him, trounced him somewhat severely for the artificiality of his literary emotions. He and I drifted asunder in the early eighties, and I rarely met him subsequently. In fact, I do not think I saw him at all after he had begun to publish under the name of "Fiona Macleod". It seems undoubted that the whole "Fiona Macleod" business was a pure mystification of Sharp himself, but yet there appear to have been people who profess to have seen the original "Fiona Macleod" in the flesh, at her home in the Highlands. A friend of the present writer relates that in the year 1900, in a Paris *salon* – of which the hostess, it may be mentioned, was the sister of an eminent French writer – he heard a Scotchman "of credit and renown" relate a circumstantial story of a visit he paid to "Fiona Macleod," and of her personal appearance as being that of a young and attractive woman – little more than a girl, in fact. Pressed to give details, the gentleman in question excused himself on the ground that to do so would be a breach of confidence, inasmuch as the lady wished to remain in strict seclusion until she deemed that the time had come to carry out a long-cherished plan of initiating a revival in Scottish life and literature. The statements of the guest referred to appeared to be accepted without question by the rest of the company, which included several Scotchmen. I give the fact of the party and of the reputable Scot's story for what it is worth. It should be observed that certain crankisms of the time, notably the pose of Jacobitism then fashionable, were represented amongst the circle assembled on the occasion, the *soi-disant* acquaintance of "Fiona Macleod" boasting himself an ardent Jacobite The whole history of Sharp and his double shows the facility of successfully faking a quasi-myth, even in the present day.

Quite a different man from Sharp was another well-known author I used to meet sometimes in the early eighties, to wit, Havelock Ellis. An able essayist, the interests of Havelock Ellis lay in the human sciences rather than in literature. His interesting and valuable researches into the psychology of sex were subsequently enshrined in a work of five volumes, which, in spite of its strictly scientific character, was, to the shame of those concerned, prohibited in this country, and had to seek a publisher in America. Besides this monumental work on the subject, Havelock Ellis, as is well known, is the author of various books and articles dealing with the interpretation and analysis of the sexual impulse in Man, in the protean forms in which it manifests itself. Ellis is in appearance and manner the type of the quiet and laborious student. He was, I believe, at one time engaged to be married to Olive Schreiner, now Mrs. Cronwright Schreiner, of South African fame, but the engagement was broken off.

As regards Ellis's special subject of investigation, nothing can surely well be more absurd or anachronistic in the modern world than the notion held by many persons, who ought to know better, that a ring fence should be drawn round this subject, not only as regards the freedom of its treatment in imaginative literature, but as to the publication of the results of purely scientific investigation. To ignore or exclude an important branch of practical human psychology from the research of the scientist, merely on the ground that the bare recital of the facts connected therewith may possibly offend the morbid delicacy of certain unwholesome people, is to head back progress just as much as it would be to discourage or prohibit (in the manner of the Church and Galileo) the publication of the results of scientific research in any other depart ment of knowledge. Yet this is precisely the attitude that certain members of the English judiciary took up as regards the researches of Havelock Ellis – thereby affording one more instance of the essentially obscurantist and reactionary role played by the High Court Bench in the national life.

In respect to the reactionary character of the wearers of ermine, and of the sort of quasi-divinity that doth hedge a judge in the estimation of that stolid and patient ox the British public, the national intelligence does not seem to have changed so very much within the last two or three generations. But that the national character as well as the national physiognomy within the

183

last fifty years of the nineteenth century has altered considerably, I have the evidence of an aged American gentleman who came over to England in 1901, and shortly after his arrival paid me a visit. This gentleman, whose name was Hinton, had been one of the friends and companions of John Brown in the Harper's Ferry incident of 1857. He wrote a history of the whole affair in an interesting book with which he presented me. What, however, especially struck me in his conversation was not so much his American reminiscences, as the astonishment he repeatedly expressed at the total change he found as between the English people of 1901 and the English people of 1848, fifty-three years before, which was the date of his last visit to this country. He had lived, it should be said, in the meantime, in a part of the United States where he had had little opportunity of meeting Britishers, either emigrants or casual visitors. According to his statement, the change was not confined merely to obvious things, such as dress, outward customs, etc., but extended to the physiognomy of the people and their natural ways and manners. The first walk, he said, that he took down the Strand on revisiting England, looking into the faces of the crowds he met, was a revelation to him. The men and women he saw appeared to him like another race from the men and women he had cast his eyes upon in a similar walk down the Strand a little more than half a century before. This was to me very interesting, as illustrating the impressions of one who had not had his perception of the difference of two generations blunted by passing through the observation of the intervening stage: leading up to the change he found.

Among the random reminiscences and reflexions in which I am taking the liberty of expanding myself in this chapter, I should not forget one or two amusing incidents in connexion with the London correspondent of a certain Italian newspaper, when he was in England. My Italian friend was one of the jolly-goodfellow sort, but possessed withal of a guileless disposition, which was taken advantage of at times by friends for the purpose of practical jokes, and by others for more sordid objects. One night, after having just cashed a cheque for five pounds in the club to which I belonged, and of which he was also a temporary member, he bought some evening journals at the corner of the Strand, handing, as he thought, five halfpennies to the newspaper boy. No sooner had he boarded his omnibus, however, than it occurred to him that he had had no money, and had for that reason cashed a cheque, with the conclusion that he had paid five pounds for his evening papers. Springing hastily from the omnibus, and rushing wildly back to the newspaper-selling corner, he found to his intense surprise that the boy was gone! On another occasion, after a convivial evening with some friends in the neighbourhood of Fleet Street, one of them kindly offered to put him in a cab to take him home to Bloomsbury. Our guileless one, who, as may be supposed, had partaken of a few whiskies in the course of the evening, fell off to sleep, and awoke anon to the consciousness of the fact that the cab-drive was an unusually long one for his destination. His attempted remonstrances with the cabman brought no result beyond the assertion that it was all right. Finally the cab drew up at the entrance to Finchley cemetery! The consternation of our journalist may be better imagined than described on the cabman's asseveration that he had been instructed to drive there by the gentleman who had hired him.

An incident recalls itself that occurred to me in connexion with this same Italian friend, which serves to illustrate the part imagination may play in an apparently plain and obvious matter. I had arranged with the friend in question to leave the club and walk up the Strand with him, but as I was detained in the club later than I expected, he proposed I should meet him in a quarter of an hour's time at the Strand telegraph office, where he was about, according to his custom, to dispatch his evening wire to Italy. Having finished what I was doing, I accordingly walked straight to the Strand telegraph office and inquired by name for our friend, who was known there, but was told to my surprise that he had not as yet called in that evening. The reason, I subsequently learnt, was that he had been taken aside by an acquaintance as he was about to leave the club, and had been detained by him in conversation some minutes, during which I, unknown to him, had left. But the sequel is interesting. I learnt the next day from him that a few minutes later than myself on the previous evening he had duly been at the telegraph office, and inquired whether any one had called there asking for him. The clerk replied that there had been only one gentleman, and that a few minutes previously. The gentleman in question, he said, was Italian in appearance, and spoke very broken English! A promising illustration this of auto-suggestion for the psychologist!

Many frequenters of the Athenaeum will recall the figure of old Stuart Glennie, author of sundry books on anthropology and the philosophy of history. Glennie was an old member of that distinguished literary centre. A typical old Highlander, this side-line relic of the Stuarts was not an unattractive personality, albeit intellectually he was not specially strong. In intention he was excellent, in general a good Socialist, and a keen student of history and the origin of institutions; but the ideas which he elaborated in a some what heavy and laborious style were not in themselves very original. Their main purport had been expressed before, and in many cases better expressed. Nevertheless, there are to be found in his writings, here and there, *aperçus* and suggestions on the subject of the general movement of history that are not altogether to be despised, His was an active mind, though of indifferent quality. In appearance and style, Glennie gave the impression of the old *gaillard*. Shaw has related to me how he met him in Trafalgar Square at the proclaimed meeting of November 21, 1887, and how in the middle of a conversation he, suddenly pointing with his umbrella to a movement in the crowd in another part of the square, charged off in that direction, as Shaw expressed it, "just as one of his ancestors might have done at Culloden."

Among the recruits to Socialism in England which the

new century brought with it, a prominent figure was the Countess of Warwick. Lady Warwick had always taken a keen interest in the Education question, the feeding of the children at school, etc., but it was not, I believe, before the opening of the twentieth century that she definitely declared herself a Socialist, and joined the Social Democratic Federation. Her entry into the movement was followed by a fête she gave to the London members of the body one Sunday in the Summer of 1905 at Easton Lodge, Essex, of which all present, I have no doubt, retain most agreeable recollections. I can well remember the occasion, and the democratic spirit in which this and a similar entertainment given a few years later were carried out as regards all the arrangements. Still more interesting personally are my remembrances of a week-end houseparty at Easton Lodge, at which myself and my wife were guests, in company with Hyndman, the late Walter Crane, Hunter Watts, and their wives, and of the discussions on matters political and social which took place during our stay. Lady Warwick's generosity towards individual members of the party is too well known to need enlarging upon here. Her genuine enthusiasm in all she undertakes sometimes leads her to underrate the difficulties in the carrying out of her intentions, but the disinterestedness which she has shown in attaching herself publicly to movements from which she has nothing personal, in the shape of material advantage or social or political kudos, to gain, must always entitle her to the esteem of all democrats.

The old school of Radicals of the Cobden-Bright period, the advanced men of the sixties and seventies, formed a well marked type, intellectually and otherwise. The very advanced ones were to be found during these decades in the Dialectical Society, a London Debating Club founded in the sixties for independent discussion of all questions. Although this rule was fairly well adhered to, there were certain sets of opinions which came specially to flourish among the members of the Society, and which were characteristic of the extreme Radicalism of the period, of which Neo-Malthusianism, as the movement for the limitation of families was called, was a conspicuous instance. The late Dr. Charles Drysdale was the chief protagonist of the view that poverty sprang from large families, and that the reduction of offspring, universally practised, would, if not precisely usher in the millennium, at least bring us halfway towards it. The notion sounds funny today, but at that time it was almost an article of faith amongst advanced Radicals, and was accepted as a self-evident proposition by almost all the member of the Dialectical Society. Secularism, in the cruder form which obtained in the ranks of popular freethought at the time, was also largely represented in the Society, of which Charles Bradlaugh and Annie Besant were prominent members. Shaw also was a frequent attendant at the bi-monthly meeting, which took place in the later period of its existence at Langham Hall, Great Portland Street. The Society was rather an odd mixture. While it was not infrequently addressed by men of eminence in their several department, and in its membership were to be found some persons of good intellectual standing, it was largely composed of intelligent self-educated, middle-class men and women. I believe it finally ceased to exist somewhere at the end of the eighties, though I do not know the precise date or circumstances of its ultimate fate. The last meeting I attended must have been somewhere about 1887. It was held in a hall off Holborn, if I remember rightly. I was the lecturer of the evening, and delivered an address traversing the pretensions of Feminism, Shaw being in the chair. This was the last I knew of it directly, though I believe it dragged on an existence for some time longer.

Talking of the Dialectical Society and the old school of Radicals reminds me of a prominent member of the Society referred to in an earlier chapter – of a man who was of some mark in journalism and the journalistic side of literature in his day, Fox Bourne. He was at one time editor of the **Examiner**, in which capacity, it should be said, he was strenuous in carrying out those principles of free discussion and just judgment of unpopular causes which he had advocated all his life. He was also the author of a **Life of John Locke** in two volumes, which, as he himself admitted, was open to adverse criticism, and in fact was not altogether a literary success. But the work for which Fox Bourne will be best remembered was as the founder and secretary and the leading spirit of the Aborigines' Protection Society. He was untiring in his advocacy of the claims of native races against the European exploiter and the military martinet acting in the service of the exploiter. Fox Bourne's intentions in this matter were admirable, and if he failed in some cases to do all he might have done, it was often owing to his not understanding the true nature of the Capitalism whose interest it is to exploit backward races and seize their land. For though, as I incidentally mentioned in a former chapter, he was at one time a frequent visitor at Karl Marx's house, he never understood the meaning of modern scientific Socialism. I knew him well, especially in his later years, and, agreeable as he was, I always found him hidebound in the ideas of the old individualistic middle-class Radicals of the mid-Victorian period. Not long before his death, I dined with him and the late Roger Casement at a West End London Club. The unfortunate Roger Casement, it should be said, was at that time doing good work in connexion with the Congo. My impression of Fox Bourne will remain as that of an eminently sincere, just, and consistent man, but one whose mind was unadaptable to new ideas, and whose outlook consequently remained throughout his later life extremely limited

Another man who was one of the founders of the Dialectical Society, and a constant and prominent figure there in its halcyon days, was J.H. Levy, who used to pride himself on being an ultra-individualist. While holding in the main most of the planks of the old political Radicalism, his gospel always remained Mill's **Essay on Liberty**. His hatred of all State action, other than that of the barest and most necessary police regulation, was an obsession with him. His political faith might be summed lip in the phrase *laisser faire à outrance*. Yet, like Fox Bourne, Levy was a scrupulously tolerant person, always ready to give his opponents a fair hearing, who regarded free discussion as the first of the rights of man. He was prepared, indeed, to press this point against all comers, and on one occasion, as he told me, he got into hotwater with some of his political friends by inviting a prominent Socialist to state his case, at one of a series of meetings organized by a well-known Liberal club, against the wishes of some of the members of the organizing committee, of which he acted as secretary. Levy, it may be said, left the impression upon all who knew him, friends and foes alike, of a man of thorough sincerity in word and deed. As a matter of fact, he devoted his life, without fee or reward, to the promulgation of the theories he believed in.

About the year 1886, R.B. Cunninghame Graham began to come prominently before the British public as an advanced democratic leader. Unlike Stuart Glennie, who sprang from a side branch of the Stuarts, Cunninghame Graham, I believe, as the great-grandson of the Earl of Monteith who took part in the Jacobite Rebellion of '15, can claim descent from the direct line of Stuart ancestry. His picturesque appearance, recalling as some say Vandyke's Charles the First, and others a Spanish hidalgo of the sixteenth century, contributed undoubtedly to spread his fame. A fluent speaker, though hardly a brilliant orator, Graham soon found himself in the forefront of the democratic and Socialist movement of the latter years of the nineteenth century, but somehow or other, after his first few years of public life, he never made any further headway as a popular leader or as a political influence. Defeated at the General Election of 1892, he largely gave up active political work and devoted himself to literature. He mainly excels in shorter sketches of men and countries, in which his light touch and characteristic style have given him a well-earned success. Socially, Cunninghame Graham is the most charming of men, but there is one point in his character which has been adversely animadverted upon by some of his best friend, and that is his passion for fashionable dress. He never appears, or at least I and others have never seen him, either in public or in private, save in the latest most superb Bond street cut, with material to match, and this has given the profane cause to make allusions to the "tailor's block." This passion for playing the part of the sartorial figure is perhaps less excusable, seeing that our friend Graham is the happy possessor of a striking face and figure, such as would assert itself in any costume, even the simplest, to the advantage of the wearer.

Speaking of Cunninghame Graham leads me to recall a friend of his, a strange Scotchman, whose name, if I remember rightly, was Stirling, who wrote a weird book, published anonymously, entitled **The Canon**, which I can best describe as a quasi-mystical interpretation of certain principles the author found running through the history of architecture. The book I reviewed at some length at the time in the **Daily Chronicle**. This man, who led a lonely life in lodgings off the south side of the Strand, appeared suddenly to take on illusions as to being persecuted by certain females on the ground of his alleged attentions to some girl or other. Not having seen him for some time after the interview in which he had disclosed his fears in this connexion, myself and a friend, who also knew him decided to call at his address and inquire if he were away or ill. The servant who opened the door at first gave somewhat evasive replies to our inquiries. She subsequently admitted, however, that Stirling was no longer living, going on to tell us that his letters had accumulated for fully a week before his closed and locked bedroom door; and when at last an entrance was forcibly effected, poor Stirling was found stretched out on the bed, dead, with his throat cut.

I will conclude the present chapter with the name of a man whose personality has a double interest. His life-long championship, through good report and through evil report, of Internationalism and anti-patriotism, as patriotism is understood to-day, is well known. The name of Felix Moscheles is familiar in connexion with the International Peace and Arbitration Association. A special interest also attaches to Felix Moscheles as the son of the eminent pianist and composer of pianoforte music, Ignaz Moscheles, and as the godson of Felix Mendelssohn Bartholdy, whose forename he bears. The aged and refined face and figure of Felix Moscheles (he is eighty-four at the time of writing) is one to impress itself on the memory. Age has certainly not staled his enthusiasm in the cause to which he has devoted his life. The journal **Concord**, which he edits and largely writes, in conjunction with the secretary of the Peace Association, Mr. J.F. Green, is evidence of this. Many are the anecdotes Moscheles has to tell of the music and musicians of the first half of the nineteenth century, especially of his father's closest friend, Mendelssohn; but as these are mostly recorded in his own autobiographical memoirs, it would be superfluous to reproduce them here. He has taken great interest in collecting and preserving mementoes of the older classical composers, possessing autograph scores, besides numbers of letters from the great German masters of the, early nineteenth century. A particularly precious relic is a curl from the head of Beethoven, with whom his father as a young man was acquainted. Felix Moscheles's pleasantest recollections of his days as an art student in Paris connect themselves with Rossini, at whose house at Passy he was a frequent visitor. Meyerbeer, I believe, he also knew. He speaks of Auber as a somewhat disagreeable man socially, and says that this was also the opinion of his father and Mendelssohn. I should not forget to mention Moscheles's gifts as an artist. While his "genre" painting is sufficiently striking, it will be probably on his skill as a portrait-painter that his future fame will rest. He has in tnis branch a singular faculty of reproducing the finest shades of expression in his sitters. His portraits of Mazzini, of George Jacob Holyoake, of the late William Clarke, the journalist, and many more, afford evidence of what is said.

# XI. When the War Came

In considering the attitude of the world in July 1914, one irresistibly recalls the passages in the Gospels referring to the advent of the expected Messiah: "Two men shall be in the field, two women shall be grinding at the mill," etc. This idea of the daily round, and the utter unexpectedness of a catastrophic event, was certainly realized in the Summer days of July 1914. Those who gave the European situation more than a cursory thought were few indeed among the general public. One day, about the middle of July, I was walking across Piccadilly Circus with an intimate friend, a well-known London publisher, when on the latter making some observation upon some current political topic, probably the Irish Home Rule question, I replied that all that was of no immediate interest or importance, but what really mattered was what was passing in Central and Eastern Europe, where the situation seemed to be big with stupendous events. My friend expressed surprise at the time, as he had not been particularly following the course of international politics recently, but he has more than once reminded me of the circumstance, which I had almost forgotten, during the last two years. As it was with this cultured and active-minded man, so it was, only very much more so, with the average British man or woman. The political horizon of the British public was bounded by Ulster, Sir Edward Carson, and Home Rule. The social and domestic horizon was filled by the usual round of business and summer interests, weekends, cricket, prospective holiday arrangements. I can well remember having occasion to call on relations on the afternoon of the eventful Saturday, the 1st of August, itself. I found them preparing to go to a cricket match! No interest, in fact, in the European crisis was visible with the general British public before the last week in July, when the possibility of the great upheaval seemed quite suddenly to dawn on this unimaginative intellectual element. It was on the Wednesday in the week in question that one first noticed anxious faces, groups discussing the question, and public interest generally aroused. Even then, as above shown, it was only partial. There were plenty of circles still obtuse to the actualities.

On Sunday, the 2nd of August, I attended the great Peace demonstration in Trafalgar Square, to which Socialist bodies, Radical clubs, and Trades Unions sent their delegations. The meeting was well attended, the Square being nearly full, but during the proceedings the boys appeared with the "specials" announcing the violation of the Luxemburg territory. Little attention was paid to the speakers, and there seemed to be a feeling of unreality about the whole proceedings. Everybody seemed to feel that the die was cast, and that the exhortations to peace amounted to little more than idle talk. As the meeting was being brought to a close, a heavy shower of rain hastened the dispersal of the crowds, and in a few minutes I found myself in the vestibule of my club, where numbers of members and their friends, fresh from the Square, had already taken refuge. Suspense and excitement were on all faces that Sunday evening. The sound of half-suppressed conversation made itself everywhere heard.

The next day, the Monday, which was Bank Holiday, I received from my son in Paris a letter stating that he was trying to get away, as Paris was no longer safe to remain in. Hurrying to town to ascertain as far as possible what routes were open, I noticed two or three of the customary wagonettes with their load of Bank Holiday makers bent on a day's outing is the country, but only two or three. In place of the usual Bank Holiday emptiness of the London streets, I found groups of people in the chief West End thoroughfares. Parliament Street and Whitehall were particularly noticeable in this respect. The approach to the Foreign Office was barred by the police. The club, usually deserted on an August Bank Holiday, was as full as the streets. Relieved of anxiety for my son by receiving a telegram announcing his arrival in London, I remained in the club to hear the parliamentary news read out, as it came up on the tape, to the assembled members in the smoking-room. Everybody (including the London correspondents of some German papers who had for long been temporary members of the club) was breathlessly awaiting news of the decision of the Cabinet as regards war or peace, but no decision came that day, and not before the afternoon of the following day, Tuesday, the 4th of August, with the arrival of the telegrams announcing the invasion of Belgium, was the ultimatum of the British Government proclaimed, which was to take effect the ensuing midnight. On Wednesday, the 5th of August, accordingly, all England woke up to the fact that the country was at war, not with native races in backward parts of the earth, or with the Dutch colonists of South Africa, but with the first of Europe's military Powers. Many people seemed stunned by the sudden realization of the fact. A certain panic was universal, which chiefly took the form of a dread of scarcity. All the gold possible had already been drawn out of the banks to be hoarded in private. Preposterous stores of provisions were laid in by many households against the contingency of Britain's food supply being cut off. People were in vain adjured to go about their "business as usual," but somehow or other business did not seem to be quite as usual. As will be remembered, a *moratorium* was at once proclaimed, and the banks officially closed till the Friday of that fateful first week of August. A general distraction fell upon the population, none knowing what was coming. Yet such is mankind that in a few weeks matters quieted down, and the population of the British Islands got, in some measure at least, used to the new conditions.

To follow the events of the war from this time forward would lie altogether outside the scope of the present book. During the terrible period we have traversed since that August week of 1914, I have resided partly near London, and partly, and indeed for longer periods, in the South of France. Thus I have had the opportunity of watching the effect of the course of events on the psychology of both the British and the French Populations. Of the former it is perhaps as yet too early to form any generalizations, but as regards the latter there is one change as compared to the traditional behaviour of the French temperament which cannot fail to strike every one at a glance. Hitherto, in national crises, and in none more than in the war of 1870, nothing has been more noticeable than the continued recurrence of gusts of excitement and panic. *Nous sommes trahis* was the cry on the occasion of every slight reverse, or absence of actual success. Men fancied spies everywhere. A state of nerves was chronic in the population. To-day, how very different the aspect of affairs! The impression gained by me in the course of a residence in both countries during the war is that of the two populations the British was more "nervy" than the French. The quiet, solid reasonableness with which the French population has behaved during the present crisis is the more remarkable in contrast to what it has been on former occasions, when one considers the fact of the occupation of a considerable section of French territory by the invader. Such a contrast is surely noteworthy, even if we discount the effects of the change in the French military system since the last war. Another point worth mention is the altered aspect of the French town, including Paris, since the war. The proverbial French gaiety has disappeared from the surface of things. The bands on the terraces of the cafés, so familiar to the residents and visitors of French towns, were no longer to be seen or heard after the outbreak of hostilities. Similarly, closed theatres, and the absence of all forms of public entertainment, was the rule. In the early period of the war even the terraces of the cafes themselves were abolished in some towns, no one being served except inside. These and sundry other severities in public manners, however, were subsequently relaxed. But all the same the traditional lightheartedness, and, as unkind British critics of the Puritan persuasion used to have it, the "frivolity" of the French temperament, has certainly been nowhere in evidence since the war began.

I have spoken of the aspect on the eve and on the outbreak of the war. In Paris, as I heard from my son on his arrival in

London, there had been no very serious apprehension on the part of the people at large, till the Saturday, the 1st of August, when the fateful declaration came from Berlin. Thereupon the panic was indescribable, and not least among the foreign population, who were given twenty-four hours to leave Paris without formalities. But the difficulty was the money question. There was no change to be got anywhere. All the silver seemed to have disappeared as if by magic. The rush of the eager, clamouring crowds at all the great railway termini to obtain tickets, where no change was given, can hardly be imagined. The lucky ones who succeeded in boarding the trains counted themselves happy if they could squeeze into a guard's van or on to a goods truck.

But what of the provincial towns of France lying on the eastern and north-eastern frontier, in the way of the threatening invasion? As an illustration of this a friend resident in Rheims has kindly furnished me with the following particulars

"The opinion generally expressed in Rheims was that some means would be found to avoid war. One of my friends called to the colours, on departing, said, 'Don't worry: it's only a false alarm; I'll be back in a few days.' Poor fellow, he never will come back.

"The mobilization order was posted up on the first day of August, and strangers had to report themselves at the Town Hall. On going there, we found the great courtyard full of a seething mass of humanity. It took many days to deal with all these foreigners, and the people of Rheims were amazed to see how many enemy aliens were living in their midst. The authorities seemed very determined to rid the town of them all, and no permits to stay were given. This gave rise to some sad scenes. I remember noticing an intelligent-looking Hungarian, who was parted from his children and their French mother, for want of the legal knot. He was an

197

enemy alien and must go; his family were French and must remain. We left him weeping bitterly.

"About this time we saw the departure of several battalions of a famous regiment of the first line of defence. The first battalion left near midnight, almost secretly. There was no enthusiasm, hardly a spectator. They marched along, silent and grave. There was no flinching, and there would be none, though they were marching to their doom.

"It may not be historically correct to describe England as taking France's part, but that is how her declaration of war against Germany was construed. The effect was magical; foreboding gave place to confidence. So the departure of the second battalion was marked by scenes of enthusiasm, The soldiers were decked out in flowers. Their tread was martial. Courage and determination seemed to radiate from their ranks. The contrast between these two scenes made a profound impression on me.

"The prompt answer of the nation to the call to arms was grand. All classes of society, from working men to learned professors, might be seen in those terrible red trousers which, it is said, cost the French troops such heavy losses in the early months of the war. I did not hear of one 'conscientious objector,' though there can have been no illusion as to the deadly nature of the ordeal before them.

"Opinions as to the result of the war fluctuated a good deal. We had no official news of French disasters, and were easily elated by the great Servian victories, and by the Russian advance, which would land our allies so soon in Berlin. But whatever elation those distant victories provoked soon gave way, before the steady advance of the German armies on Paris, to a feeling of hopelessness. 'What can we do against such desperate odds?' people asked. And when the Germans occupied our town, many said to me, 'I suppose we are Prussians now!' or words to that effect. There was a feeling of despair – that all was lost, and that nothing remained, as even the most sanguine people said, but to make peace, pay an indemnity as in '70, and wipe the slate clean again.

"The town was administered admirably by the Mayor, who was quite the man of the hour, and who formed committees to regulate every branch of the town's activities. Coin had disappeared from circulation; it was replaced by paper money, the smallest coupon being 25c. (2d.). The prices of the principal articles of food were fixed, and so there was no rise.

"Towards the end of August, Belgian soldiers who had escaped from Namur began to arrive. Then for days there was a steady stream of refugees pouring in from Mezieres and that region. These people were of all ages and conditions. Most of them bore bundles on their backs or pushed baby-carriages loaded with a heterogeneous array of ill-assorted household goods – clocks, frying-pans, clothes, crockery, all thrown together pell-mell, testifying to their hasty flight before the dreaded German invasion. In the last degree of exhaustion, they presented a most forlorn picture of 'man's inhumanity to man.' For ten terrible days they had tramped along the highways, living for the most part on what raw roots they could scratch up as they passed along, sinking by the roadside when they could drag themselves no farther. How the children survived I do not know.

"Rheims gave them the kindliest welcome. They were housed, fed, and comforted, and then sent on, it was said, to the South of France. Some of them had terrible tales to tell of butchery and burnings, but most of them had their faculties too blunted by what they had gone through to give any account of themselves.

"On September 3rd seven Uhlans rode in and established themselves at the Town Hall. Next day staff officers of the Saxon Army arrived, and while they were closeted with the Mayor the town was violently bombarded. The Saxons accused the Mayor of treachery, and threatened terrible reprisals. It is already a matter of history how the Mayor proved conclusively, from fragments, that the shells were German ones, and thus saved the town from one of those scenes of bloody reprisals which characterized the German advance through Belgium and France.

"Apart from this tragic event, the Saxon domination was bearable. Their requisitions, it is true, were on a vast scale. This organized robbery was evidently part of their campaign of 'frightfulness.' But the courage, energy, and diplomacy of the Mayor and his coadjutors conjured every peril.

"The Saxon soldiery, speaking generally, were correct in their behaviour. What they bought they paid for in cash. I heard of very little thieving. Some of them could speak a little French, and made friendly advances to the inhabitants. I heard one of them explaining, with many gestures, that the Saxons were not Prussians, whom they detested – they were 'Saxon-Englisch.' Another drew a coin from his pocket, and tapping the effigy of the Kaiser with his finger, exclaimed, 'Lui, très mauvais!'

"The officers were arrogant and highhanded. Every day saw some new proclamation threatening death for any breach of its regulations. They were also accused of plundering the houses they were billeted in. I was not brought much in contact with them, but found them polite enough.

"The Saxon occupation lasted barely ten days. On

retreating, they carried off about one hundred hostages, whose names were posted up, and a proclamation announced that they would all be hanged if the army were molested in its retreat. However, they came back safely, and reported that the commander had expressed his satisfaction with the conduct of the town, and promised that it should not be again bombarded. If he meant this as a joke, it was a grim one, for that same night the first shells of a bombardment that has already lasted more than two years (October 1916) fell on the town, and the destruction of the Cathedral of Rheims quickly followed this deceptive promise.

"The bombardment which marked the entry of the victors made over one hundred victims. When. first saw those horribly mutilated and mangled bodies, lying in great pools of blood, all feelings of pity and compassion were swamped by the physical repulsion and nausea that overpowered us. Our one desire was to get away, and it required a tremendous effort to remain and render aid where it could be of any avail. As the recurrent bombardments inured us to the sight of death, I observed a change in our mental attitude. We no longer sought to avoid the ghastly sights resulting from German 'frightfulness,' but rather felt a morbid curiosity as to what had happened, and this developed into something like callousness. I do not think we felt less sorrow for suffering, but a certain numbness of sensation had befallen us. Yet we did not lose all capacity for emotion. 'We were living under the constant menace of a sudden and horrible death, and the ruthless and barbarous slaughter of so many innocent people, mostly old men, women, and children, aroused intense indignation. Anger, keen and vehement, was openly expressed, and the Kaiser would have received a short shrift had he fallen into our hands.

"Our only refuge from the shells was the cellars of the great champagne houses. It is difficult to give you a clear impression, in a few words, of life in those cellars. Imagine several hundred people, congregated in groups, lying on straw or boxes, on a cement flooring, fifty or sixty feet below ground, in semi-darkness, for there was but a candle every dozen yards or so. Little food but bread. No hot meals, though the manager made them tea as long as his stock lasted. Sanitary arrangements improvised in the most primitive manner. Many of the people never washed themselves, judging by appearances. The predominant emotion, fear, finding vent in vociferous apostrophes to the Deity, especially in moments of panic. It was a nightmare from which we were glad to escape when occasion at last offered. We found the quiet and tranquillity of Paris strange after the noise and devastation of Rheims. Nothing would induce us to repeat our experiences. But we shall not readily forget the dark champagne cellars, nor the kindness of those in charge of them."

A noteworthy fact in connexion with the earlier period of the war was the ignorance in which both the French and British public were kept as to the course of events. Had they known of the great defeat, reported as a "check," of the French Army between Metz and Strasburg, towards the end of August, or of the rout of Rennenkampf's army in East Prussia, a few days later, also reported as a "check," of the full extent of the reverses at Mons and Charleroi, or of the full significance of the march on Paris, there might have been something like a panic in both countries. The second week of September the battle of the Marne of course altered the face of the situation. But no one for weeks after realized the true import of the change consequent on that event, from the "war of movement" to the "war of positions." Up to this time the hostilities had been conducted pretty much on the accustomed lines of warfare – the sending out of scouts, followed by the advance of armies, engagements in the field, strategic manoeuvrings, etc. From the middle of September onward the course of affairs began to change, till before another month had elapsed they had assumed quite another character, and one that may fairly be said to have been unknown to the wars of previous European history. Though in all warfare entrenchment has been an incident, yet it has been no more than a local incident, a matter of hours or at most of days. In the present war the case is quite different. Here entrenchment is the central fact of the war, the main factor on which the whole course of hostilities has turned, after the first two or three months of the campaigns on the various fronts. The causes of this great revolution in the conditions of warfare is of course a highly interesting subject of inquiry, but one which only a technically equipped and competent authority on military matters can effectively handle. One consequence of the change is, however, sufficiently noticeable to the layman. Trench warfare on a great scale, as at present, would seem indefinitely to prolong a campaign by rendering decisive engagements highly improbable, where not impossible. In trench warfare a Waterloo or a Sedan is scarcely conceivable. The section of a line even seriously broken does not by any means necessarily imply a disastrous defeat for the army in question, which by judicious retreat and reconstitution of its line may quite well continue to operate as if nothing had happened to it, provided it has sufficient reserves. In former wars things were quite otherwise.

The earlier stages of the war are remarkable for having been the soil on which originated among English people two thoroughgoing and elaborate myths of the approved antique pattern. The first of these was the stories of the angels at Mons, and the second the wide-spread, and for a few days the almost universally accredited, report of the huge Russian army landed in Scotland, and sent down south to check the German advance on Paris. The angels at Mons, of course, had the usual vouchers in

203

the shape of personal witnesses which are forthcoming wherever the supernatural is in question. Valiant British soldiers, as was alleged, swore to having seen something not of this earth, though as to precisely what it was the accounts varied. One version had it that it was a legion of angels that held up the German advance and saved the British battalions ; with others, it was the solitary figure of St. George on horseback, as impressed on the five-shilling piece. In deference to the French allies, there were, I think, one or two variants which identified the celestial visitation with the figure of St. Michael, and, if I remember rightly, of Jeanne d'Arc. According to the opinion of many persons the whole thing arose out of a little feuilleton by Mr. Arthur Machen in the **Evening News,** though there were others who strenuously denied this, alleging the reports in question to have originated before Mr. Machen's article appeared, and in any case quite independently of it. Be this as it may, among those who professed to believe the story were at least one popular Nonconformist minister, and, if I mistake not, two or three other members of the clerical profession well known to the public.

The other myth referred to bore no overt relatiou to the supernatural, but presented all the characteristics of a true myth, notwithstanding. Here also the origin of the astounding report was untraceable. There was not even a Mr. Machen or a newspaper statement to fall back upon. The story of the Russian army landed in Scotland spread like wildfire from mouth to mouth among the public before it even got into the newspapers. Of this there is no question. People had seen blinded trains at various junctions and had caught a glimpse of undoubted Cossacks peering out of railway compartment windows. The evidence was such, indeed, as to deceive the very elect of true British caution and common sense.

As already indicated, I was living near London when the war broke out, and remained there till the beginning of December, when circumstances urged me to go to Paris, partly for family reasons, and partly as a stage towards seeking my *appartement* in Nice, for considerations of health, during the winter months. Travelling on the Continent just then was generally regarded as an unpleasant business. Many had been the stories told in the papers, during those early months of the war, of trains held up and their occupants turned out into some temporary shed, to make room for convoys of wounded; of other trains run into sidings and left there for hours, or it might be a day or two, with their passengers, in order to leave the line clear for the; transport of troop. This being so, most civilians were disinclined to hazard their luck in crossing the Channel, an undertaking itself regarded as more or less risky, owing to the danger of submarines. Nevertheless, accompanied by my wife and my friend the London publisher before alluded to, I went, albeit with certain misgivings of what might happen, this being my first experience of travelling, in war-time, through a tract of country that had been partially occupied by hostile troops not more than three months before, and which was still within comparatively short distance of the battle-front. However, beyond an unpleasant and tempestuous Channel crossing, nothing happened. The journey from Boulogne to Paris by way of Beauvais, the railway viaduct near Amiens, blown up by the Germans, not having as yet been rebuilt, passed off without incident, though it necessarily took some two hours longer than by the usual route.

We found Paris itself quiet and wonderfully dark on our arrival. The next day further showed us a city chastened by adversity, but no signs of excitement or panic of any kind. The Boulevards looked, indeed, somewhat deserted as compared with ordinary times, but the restaurants and cafes were open as usual. My friend and myself having accomplished what we had to do in Paris, we started by the night train for the South, where we arrived, also without having encountered any incident suggestive of wartime, the following afternoon. It is interesting to note that, contrary to the experience of others at the time we are referring to, we were not challenged for our "papers" in Paris or on the journey.

205

The winter of 1914-15 was naturally a gloomy one for the Mediterranean town. At Nice the opera house was closed, and the theatres likewise, leaving a few "cinemas" as the only form of popular entertainment to be indulged in. There was one thing, however, which agreeably distinguished the Mediterranean littoral from the places in the North nearer the seat of war. There was no restriction as to lighting beyond what municipal parsimony, encouraged by the absence of visitors, suggested. For the rest, the dreary monotony of the daily bulletins of trenches taken, lost, or retaken, told on the spirits of the genial children of the South, no less than on those of less favoured climes.

In dealing with the war, every Socialist is naturally brought up against the fact of the treachery to the fundamental principles of Socialism, as well as to International party ties, on the part of the Social Democratic members of the Reichstag. When we consider that but a few days before the outbreak of the war, both at the meeting of the International Socialist Bureau at Brussels and, on the part of certain of the leaders at least, a day or two subsequently in Paris, the strongest assurances were given by members of the present majority of the Reichstag "fraction" that the German proletariat would never consent to fight their French brethren, and that the party members in the Reichstag would never vote war credits for the Government – when we consider this, the action of these very same men, and of the colleagues in whose name they spoke, scarcely more than a week later, must constrain the mildest and most indulgent critic to admit that history can hardly show-a baser and a viler instance of treachery and broken pledges than their conduct. Of course, writing as I am before the end of the war, when most of what is going on in Germany is hidden from the view of the outer world, it would be unfair to assume that the majority of the Social Democratic Party throughout the country ought to be regarded as in any way accomplices in this act of treachery. Until a party Congress can be held at which all members of the party, those now at the front no less than those at home, can be represented and speak their minds freely through their delegates, we have no right to assume that the majority of the party in the country is in sympathy with the majority of the present Reichstag representation. We know, as a matter of fact, that the followers of Karl Liebknecht are numerous throughout Germany, but we do not know how numerous, or what proportion they represent to the other sections of the party. One thing is certain, however, and that is that, outside Germany, no one calling himself a Socialist should consent again to meet in Congress or to hold any intercourse whatsoever, either directly or indirectly, with traitors to the principles of Socialism, to the International Socialist Party, and to Humanity, such as the "majority" of the present representation of the Social Democratic Party in the German Reichstag.

It does not lie within the scope of this chapter, as conceived by the author, to provide one more of the fancy sketches of the political reconstruction of Europe with which the British public has been regaled since the beginning of the war. It behoves all friends of progress and peace to look to it that the European democracy is not cheated, by any secret understanding among the governing classes of the *Entente* States, of the full attainment of that object which has been so often officially proclaimed as that for which we are fighting – to wit, the extinction of Prussia as an independent Military Power, and the reconstitution of the German States on the basis of equality in a loose federal bond, the necessary consequence of this. We may be good pro-Allies, but it is well for us not to forget that governing classes are governing classes all the world over, have interests in common against the democracy, and that, as William Morris was fond of saying, "Dog doesn't eat dog!" Into the details of the actual reconstruction after the war it is in my opinion premature to enter at the present time of writing.

The effect of the war upon the Socialist movement more or less in all, but especially in belligerent, countries has had its repercussion in Great Britain in the split in the British Socialist Party, and the foundation of a rival organization, the National

Socialist Party, by a large and growing section of British Socialists, comprising, almost to a man, all the surviving "old guard" of the pioneer Socialist body of this country, the old original Social Democratic Federation.

From the beginning of the war was visible an inevitable tendency to scission between partisans of a "peace at any price," even at the price of leaving Prussian despotism and Prussian militarism intact, to continue to terrorize Europe and start another war probably in less than ten years' time, and those who wished to see the military monarchies of Central Europe destroyed once for all, and who cherished the hope at least that the present war, the most terrific in the world's history, may prove to be the last war, at least on a large scale. Those who take this view regard the *Entente* Powers as acting simply in the capacity of a politico-international police force to punish crime and aggression.

There is an element in the psychology of the ultra-pacifist British Socialist which must not be lost sight of. It is the acute anti-patriotic bias which reduces political and ethical judgments to an absurdity. The bias implies that because Great Britain happens to be on a particular side, that side must necessarily be in the wrong and its enemies in the right. Now, it is quite true that in the colonial wars of the nineteenth century, and last, but not least, in the Boer War which ushered in the present century, this country has almost invariably played an aggressive and criminal role as a State. Hence the moral judgment of all fair-minded and disinterested persons, with a strength of conscience sufficient to resist the "jingo" or patriotic bias, has condemned the policy of this country. In that most flagrant case, the Boer War, so much bitterness was engendered, and the moral sense of a large section of Englishmen was so much shocked by the official conduct of their country, that it is not perhaps surprising that the strength of the anti-British bias then engendered should still be operative, especially among certain sections of Radicals and Socialists who bore the heat and burden of the protest at that time. This, there is no doubt, is the underlying cause of much of the Pacifism and pro-Germanism in England to-day. It is, nevertheless, strange to find such an utter lack of logical faculty in these worthy persons that they cannot see that precisely the same moral principles which led them to execrate the action of Great Britain in the Boer War ought necessarily to lead them to execrate the action of Germany in the present war. To allow one's anti-patriotic bias to run so wild as to kick over all the bounds of ethico-political logic seems scarcely compatible with the sane mind. Yet so it is. In addition to this, of course, certain well known fallacies play their part, as, for example, the obsession alluded to by Mill in one of his chapters on Fallacies (**Logic**, vol.ii. p.351), to wit, that there must always be faults on both sides, an obsession which blinds a man to truth and justice when it is to be found on one side only, as it very often is. Another fallacy which in this as in other cases is apt to lead the ordinary man astray, is the confusion of issues. This fallacy of the untrained mind is very much in evidence amongst the pacifist and pro-German Socialists. Because Socialists have attacked all existing governments as institutions for the maintenance of the present class-State, in the interests of Capitalism and land-monopoly, it is therefore argued that we cannot take the side of the Allied States in the present war for the overthrow of the Prussian military power. Here comes in the fallacy of failing to grasp the bearings of a specific issue. The Allied Powers may have all the evil qualities in their governmental institutions, as in the economic system common to all existing States, that Socialist criticism ascribes to them, and yet they may be wholly in the right as regards the specific issue of this war. The distinction is recognized in common life. The most strenuous votary of the Nonconformist conscience would presumably not trip up a policeman while chasing a burglar, on the ground that he was a person of immoral life. In most cases, indeed, he would hardly claim it to be his duty, on the above ground, even to refuse him his active assistance to capture the burglar. He would generally have sense enough to recognize that the question of the private conduct of the policeman's life, and his act of apprehending a burglar, were two distinct and irrelevant issues. And so it is with this war. Russian despotism at home and British earth-hunger abroad do not affect the, issue of the present struggle. However bad in themselves these characteristics of the States in question may be, their policy may nevertheless be wholly justified in its resistance to Prussian aggression.

There is another thing to be observed in this connexion. Although the colonial policy and the colonial wars of England have, almost invariably, from any consistently Democratic or Socialist point of view, been infamous, yet British action in continental politics has not quite invariably been so. Thus, though the war with revolutionary France organized by Pitt in the interests of European reaction was scandalous enough, the later campaign for the overthrow of the military empire of Napoleon I was undoubtedly in the interests of the peaceful development of Europe generally, apart from any legitimate patriotic justification it may have had in removing from the country the threat of invasion. The present situation is in some respects analogous. In place of the French Empire of Napoleon Bonaparte we have the Prusso-German Empire of the Hohenzollerns. In either case the war represents the resistance of Europe to an aggressive military despotism. As to the ultimate issue of the war, the terms of peace, etc., at the time of writing it would seem futile, as already said, to enter on any discussion. I may remark, however, that I agree with my friend Jules Guesde in deprecating any far-reaching cutting-up of German territory, while holding fast by the principle of the absolute and final destruction of the military power of the Central Monarchies. The future of Germany, it seems to me, should take the form of a loose federation of the different German States, without the hegemony of any one State, with no military power beyond that of a local State militia, in general analogous to that of Switzerland, but without arty central or national directing power, or Ober-commando. This would seem to represent the general terms, the minimum conditions, under which a lasting peace with the Central Nations (I expressly forbear to say the Central Powers) could be effected.

# XII. Concluding Reflexions

In thinking back on the course of one's past life, there are obviously many interesting reflexions which are suggested.[1] One such presented itself to me recently, when I bethought me that my own personal memory-synthesis included within its purview a span of time equal to that of the whole life of Shakespeare. It was while reading the two monumental volumes on Shakespeare's England, recently published for the three-hundredth anniversary of his birth by the Clarendon Press, that I was led to recall the above circumstance. The celebration of the anniversary of Shakespeare's birth in the year 1864 I can distinctly remember. I was at Brighton as a boy at the time, and I believe was taken to hear one of the many discourses that were being delivered on the Bard of Avon in the Spring of that year. It was about the time that Garibaldi paid his celebrated visit to England and was received with the wildest demonstrations of enthusiasm. From that time to this my memory of the main flow of events is of course distinct, and more or less continuous, and it is somewhat startling to reflect that this span of time, covered by one's own mental experience, represents the whole life-period of the immortal one. Such a reflexion as the above is only one of the many to which the advance of age in oneself gives rise.

The changes in opinion and attitude in the British mind, as decade succeeded decade, and much more, of course, as generation succeeded generation, during the lifetime of the present writer, have been already dwelt upon in the course of these reminiscences. As illustrating again a remarkable change which has taken place within the present century owing to the progress of mechanical invention, I may note an incident which happened to me about the middle of the nineties, i.e. not much more than twenty years ago. I was speaking at a Socialist meeting, and on some objection being raised to a suggestion I made, on the ground of its involving difficulties of transit, or something to that effect, I replied that the problem of aerial locomotion would probably have been solved before long, and that airboats and flying-machines would not only supplement, but might even have superseded, the then existing methods of transit. It seems worth recording to-day that this remark of mine, made less than a quarter of a century ago, was greeted at the time with a roar of laughter from the audience, who evidently regarded it as the mad dream of an unpractical, scatterbrained Utopian, if not as an intentional joke. Looking back at the incident from the standpoint of to-day, one is inclined to think what fools peopled the world in the nineties. Yet we see similar instances of short-sightedness, even among people at other times the most intelligent.

The power to rise above the ruts of thought in which one has grown up is not everybody's affair. The members of my audience in the nineties lead been accustomed all their lives to the notion of flying-machines and dirigible aircraft as no better than a whimsical crankism. They had never taken the trouble to reflect on the implications of the bird's flying power, and of the quite obvious possibility of imitating and reproducing mechanically the organic conditions on which it is founded.

To take an illustration from another department. Some years ago the Socialist lecturer was constantly met by would-be wiseacres with the assertion that the stimulus of necessity, and in the last resort of hunger, was requisite to induce men to work at all, laziness being one of the fundamental characteristics of what they were pleased to term "human nature." They had heard this thesis proclaimed as an axiom, by those whom they deemed sagacious persons, from their youth up, and never having taken the trouble to look closer into the motives of men, they had come to regard any theory which ignored it as an absurdity. This is a remarkable instance of the short-sightedness of the average man, since it requires such a very little study, or even ordinary observation, of "human nature" to show that the theory is baseless. In the first place, the phrase "human nature" itself is a

212

very vague one, since in the course of man's evolution it has changed its character on so many sides. But let this pass. By "human nature" the persons in question generally mean the human nature of themselves and their neighbours, in other words, human nature as moulded by the capitalist civilization of the nineteenth and twentieth centuries. Let us then take the men and women surrounding us to-day. If we do, we shall find that in every average normal man or woman there undoubtedly exists a strain of aversion to excessive toil, yet that there is an equal aversion to absolute idleness. Find me the most leisured man without the slightest necessity of earning his livelihood who yet does not choose to work at something or other, very often of a quite unremunerative character. I don't say it is always useful work, by any means, but yet it is work, and sometimes hard work, and not idleness. Even the man who devotes himself to athletics, or to games such as football or cricket, as a serious business in life, without fee or reward, though it may be a question whether he is doing anything useful, is certainly not idle or lazy. He toils, and sometimes very hard, when there is absolutely no necessity for his doing so. Again, look around to-day at the numbers of men, some of them men of means, many of them leaving good and easy positions in their several walks of life, who have voluntarily accepted, not only the chances of death on the battlefield, but the arduous labours of the trenches, and that not merely without any prospect of material gain, but at a positive material loss to themselves. Once more, look at the hundreds of women who, equally without any stimulus of gain or economic necessity, have undertaken heavy, and in itself often unpleasant, work as nurses. And these cases are more the rule than the exception during these last three years. Oh, but, you will say, the force of public opinion drove these men and women to hard and unremunerative labour. Even if the statement be admitted up to a certain point, can those who say this be so dense as not to see that, in a society organized on a Socialist basis, an infinitely stronger force of public opinion would constrain men and women to fulfil their moderate and just share of the necessary work of the

213

world? One would not deny the existence of pathological specimens of humanity to whom all work is distasteful. But such are so exceptional as to be negligible from a practical point of view. The tendency to exaggerate their numbers by superficial and thoughtless people is due to the fact that under the present anarchic conditions of society so many men are forced by circumstances to seek their livelihood in uncongenial occupations. That such persons should show an inclination at times to shirk the uncongenial work to which circumstances have condemned them does not by any means imply that they are averse to all work. In a reasonable society this fact of "human nature" would of course be taken into account. There are few men for whom some form of useful labour is not endurable or even attractive. The thing is, in the process of the education of youth, to find out what this special form of work is. To do so is indeed one of the most important functions of educational training, though as yet this function has been entirely neglected. And even if it had not been so, the results obtained would have been largely useless under present capitalistic conditions.

One of the changes which distinguishes the present generation from those preceding is undoubtedly the tendency to a mistrust of all conventional shibboleths. The present generation is quite prepared to reconsider all positions. What would formerly have been considered paradox is the breath of its intellectual life. This tendency to paradoxism with the modern man, healthy though it be in itself, is, as I have already pointed out in a former chapter, apt at times to run to excess, as possibly in the case of Shaw and his perennial paradox-joke. Shaw undoubtedly has the signal merit of having stimulated the mind of the English-speaking peoples to independent thought and Socratic questionings, but it is doubtful whether the backwash of his influence has not tended to promote a craving for paradoxical fare intellectually, which – on the analogy of the much decried craving for alcohol, or for highly spiced condiments gustatively – has destroyed all taste intellectually for plain statements of fact, not wearing the garb of paradox. Now, this is certainly not healthy. The well-known Delphic motto "Nothing in excess" applies as much to paradox as to anything else. In fact, the excess in the case of paradox, if without measure, may well have the result on the coming generation of producing a reaction by sheer surfeit. This may for the time being obscure the good effect left by the critical spirit aroused in the existing generation, with the consequence of a general reactionary falling back on old and exploded dogmatic positions, by way of relief. Such reactions are common phenomena in history. The well-known case of the generation succeeding the French Revolution may serve, *mutatis mutandis,* as an illustration. The present generation does not fully realize that mere paradoxical brilliancy and smartness, like everything else, may pall after a time upon the intellect satiated with it.

Again, among the special fashions of the present time is the one before alluded to in passing, namely, the elevation of the nation-State into a god or object of supreme devotion, with a corresponding cult of its own, which has really, if not nominally, substituted itself for the old religious faith. Of this sentiment, which in its present form as Imperialism is traceable for thirty years or more back, and has, as one might expect, been accentuated a hundredfold by the present war, it is unnecessary to speak. In antithesis to this cult of Patriotism, now dominant, stands the Internationalist principle of Socialism. It has been often said of late that Internationalism does not mean Anti-nationalism. But if it does not mean Anti-nationalism it certainly means anti-Imperialism. And more than this, the Internationalism of the consistent Socialist certainly does imply the relegation of nationality, or race, and all that it connotes, to a place secondary to that of Humanity. In what I may term the religion of Patriotism, of which we hear so much nowadays, Humanity merely exists as a background to "one's country." The first consideration is the material aggrandizement and the moral honour and glory of the nation-State into which one has been born. This is the first consideration with modern Imperialism, which is the form in which Patriotism inevitably clothes itself, in the case of a nationality that is also a great World-Power.

The conflict between these two principles, Imperialism and Internationalism, between national material interest on the one side, as opposed to human interest with its moral sanctions on the other, can hardly fail to constitute one of the great issues of the world in the near future. I say this in the full consciousness of the fact that for the time being the principle of Internationalism seems to have suffered a defeat at the hands of its rival, convinced as I am that it is no real defeat, but merely a temporary set-back ; and furthermore, that there are many among those who are heart and soul with the cause of the Allies in the present war who are so, less on the ground of Patriotism than from a desire to see justice among peoples, and the rights of our common Humanity vindicated. Of course, for the moment, the call of Patriotism has the upper hand and dominates the world, but even now the idea of the closer union of the Allied nations, though born of antagonism and war, may later on, when present hatreds have died down, be one of the factors that will pave the way for the truer and more complete Internationalism of the future.

The present war, as the Boer War and other wars have done before, gives rise to a singular ethical problem. The moral aspects of the wars in question are, generally speaking, perfectly plain. The right and wrong of the causes of the wars, i.e. the right and wrong when judged according to ethical standards universally admitted otherwise in private life, must be obvious, one would think, to any one judging impartially on the facts. Yet how is it that men of good repute personally, and decently honourable in private life, can bring themselves in international concerns to profess publicly to justify the side of their own country, when it is not merely in the wrong, but criminally in the wrong? We have all of us known, at the time of the Boer War, Englishmen who as ordinary citizens were men of integrity, truthful and fair in their dealings, and who nevertheless pretended to justify the action of the British Government in its aggression on the two South African Republics, not to speak of the "methods of barbarism" in its conduct of the war. These men ignored, or lamely attempted by falsehoods to explain away, the admitted facts of the case. To-day we see precisely the same phenomenon in the case of Germany. Here again you have men, doubtless equally honourable in their private life and dealings, who are prepared to come forth publicly and defend an act of international brigandage, and this without one word of reprobation for the further inhuman crimes committed in carrying it out. Now, how are these things to be reconciled? The self-interest of men holding positions under government, or the party considerations of politicians, no doubt is a large, perhaps the chief, factor therein. But these merely selfish reasons would hardly suffice completely to explain the case in all instances, though they might do so in some. I think we are driven to the conclusion that a genuine psychological blindness plays its part in the matter. Some at least of these men are really affected by a kind of ethical myopia for the time being; the patriotic sentiment which they have possibly inherited, or which in any case has been hammered into them from their youth up, and has lately been taking on the aspect of a religion, has unconsciously warped their whole ethical nature. Of course, there are a large number who know well enough that their country is wrong, and only defend it from interested motives. But I believe there are also some who are not consciously dishonest in the matter and to whom the foregoing remarks will apply. This will continue to be the case, it is to be feared, until the modern religion of Patriotism is supplanted in the minds of men by the religion of Humanity, the sentiment of a common human brotherhood. Once admit Patriotism as the highest sentiment, as religion, and you have the problem of contradictory Patriotisms to deal with. When they laud Patriotism, people generally mean their own Patriotism. But how about "the other fellow's" Patriotism? How about the Prussian's, for example? If "My country right or wrong" is a noble sentiment on the banks of the Thames, how does it look on the banks of the

217

Spree?

Let us turn now to other phases of the modern mind. One of the curious things I have noted is the growth for at least a generation past in the medical profession of what I may term medical asceticism. Asceticism, it should not be forgotten, is quite as constant a phenomenon of human psychology as self-indulgence. We have before had theological asceticism, to wit, an asceticism based on the notion of the harsh treatment of the body being conducive to the welfare of the soul. This, of course, has played a great part at different periods in the Christian religion, but we find it largely supplanted at the present day by medical asceticism. The perennial ascetic bias of the human mind, feeling the theological basis of ascetic practice to be unsatisfactory and out of harmony with the general modern outlook on life, believes itself to have found a more satisfactory basis for the mortification of the flesh, not for the benefit of the soul of man, which has fallen into the background, but for the welfare of his body. Hence medical asceticism, which tends to reduce to the minimum, if not to utterly abolish, the lusts of the flesh and the sensible enjoyments of life, on physiological grounds. Take the case of alcohol. This is seen in the crusade, not of course against obvious excess, which every one condemns, but against alcohol altogether.[2] And this is only one manifestation of the tendency in question. It is the habit of the medical profession nowadays to forbid its patients, and to discourage, at least, on the part of mankind in general, the use or practice of anything conducive to the satisfaction or delight of the bodily sense. In all living, that which is conducive to the ease of the body is condemned. Not only in drinking is the mellowing influence of alcohol denounced as incompatible with bodily health, but the eating of everything that is palatable is declared noxious. Smoking is objected to, and has recently been sought to be made illegal for the young person.

As an instance of the curious ascetic phase through which the art of medicine is passing, I may mention that a friend of mine, who was suffering during the very hot weather from the condition of the skin known as "prickly heat," was seriously advised by an able medical man that he should on no account indulge in cooling and effervescing drinks! This patient, I should say, in spite of the injunction, continued to take his cooling and effervescing drinks, and the "prickly heat" symptoms went notwithstanding. It is difficult for a layman to regard the prohibition in question as anything else than a piece of medical asceticism, since it seems hardly possible that refreshing beverages, which give relief and tone to the system, can have an irritating effect on the skin. It is curious, but nevertheless undoubtedly true, that at the present day there are many among the public who would lose confidence in a doctor who did not prescribe for them something of the nature of penitential and purgatorial diet. A generation or so ago the patients expected the doctor to order them highly coloured and nauseating drugs, so much so, that I knew of a medical man who used to keep different coloured waters with a little harmless but nauseous flavouring in them, to satisfy those of his patients who did not have much the matter with them, and who did not really require any medicine at all. The same practice has prevailed, I believe, in sundry London hospitals. At a still earlier date the "patient" public thought the doctor way not doing his duty if he did not prescribe copious blood-lettings. The fashion is now all for ascetic dieting ; no alcohol, no condiments, no smoking, no anything but what is to the bodily senses of man *fade* and insipid. As regards this whole question of dietetics, a medical friend of mine told me that in a recent interview with an elderly colleague, the author of a well-known book on the subject, he expressed his serious doubts whether the whole modern theory of diet had any scientific basis to it, to which the elder man replied, "You are twenty years younger than I am, but it seems you have already come to the conclusion at which I have only just arrived myself." The obvious and common-sense view, one would think, would be, that it is for every human being to find out by experience what suits him or her best, and that diet is not a subject on which any effective rules and regulations can be laid down for general observance. Medical, like other fashions, have their day and cease to be, though sometimes, as with the bleeding mania, their passing may be slow.

The principles and propaganda of Feminism were running high in the land up to the outbreak of the war, and though for the time being undoubtedly overshadowed by the great events of the last two years, there is no reason for thinking that Feminism, theoretical and practical, will not reassert itself when the present crisis is over. In my book on the subject I have distinguished between political and sentimental Feminism. The propaganda of Feminism has for its practical object to exalt the woman at the expense of the man. We have had echoes of sentimental Feminism during the war itself, notably, as already mentioned, in the case of Edith Cavell, where we have a woman exalted to the rank of a demi-goddess of heroism, while of the Belgian architect, Philippe Bancq, who suffered at the same time, for the same offence against the German invaders of his country, not a word has been said. Compare the case of Captain Fryatt, whose murder was even more in contravention of the laws of civilized war than that of Edith Cavell, and yet we hear of no streets named after lain and no festivals in his honour! The general theory of sentimental Feminism seems to be that the shooting of one woman non-combatant outweighs the murder of ten men non-combatants. Such divinity doth hedge a female of the human species!

As regards the theoretical basis of the Feminist contention, a case has recently come under my notice which may serve to supplement the instances, as given in my book, of special pleading, and indeed of the complete perversion of scientific fact in the interest of Feminist theory. The object of the theorists of Feminism is to prove that woman is mentally the equal of man. If they can only make her out to be superior, so much the better. A Viennese professor, of Feminist proclivities, has recently, I think, fairly "taken the cake" (as the phrase goes) in this connexion. As is well known, it is the grey matter of the brain which is correlated with sensation, thought, and conscious action, while the white matter consists of nerve-strands communicating between the cell-group centres of grey matter. Hence the obvious fact that upon the quality and the amount of the grey matter depend the amount and quality of the intellect of the individual. Now, it is a further well-ascertained fact that the comparison of the brains of the average man and woman shows a vastly greater preponderance of grey to white cells in the former than in the latter. These well-authenticated, and hitherto universally admitted, scientific facts obviously constitute a very awkward stumbling-block in the way of the theory Feminists are anxious to propagate as regards sex-capacities. Accordingly, the Viennese Feminist professor spoken of decided to take the bull by the horns, and attack the well-established conclusions of science in this matter, by declaring the latter to be all wrong, the white and not the grey matter of the brain being the most important elements in its structure as correlated with the higher mental processes! Needless to say, the unbiased results of generations of research in cerebral structure and function stand now as firmly as ever they did, the unshotted broadside levelled against them by the distinguished Feminist Viennese professor notwithstanding. It is well for laymen to be on their guard against Feminist pseudo-science. That men professing to be savants can lend themselves to this species of charlatanry is nothing less than disgraceful.

The present war is affording a stalking-horse for more nostrums than one The trick is to trace the atrocities and misdeeds of the Prusso-German Government and armies to the absence in Germany of the influence of one's own particular nostrum. Thus, the Feminist will try to persuade you that the crimes of the German Army are due to defects in the German character, arising from the absence of the cultus of Woman among German men and of the emancipation of Woman in the Feminist sense in the Fatherland. The shooting of Miss Cavell and sundry outrages on women in Belgium and the North of France, we are told, are referable to an insufficient spirit of gallantry or chivalry, i.e. of kowtowing to femalehood, on the part of German men. If female suffrage and female influence generally had been present in German social and political life, it is alleged, we should have had no war, or, in case of war, no "frightfulness," and above all the sacrosanct sex would have been spared and treated with the due reverential awe which it becomes vile man to show in his dealings therewith. All this sort of talk is, I suppose, swallowed by a section of the British public at its face-value, being, as they are, utterly ignorant of the facts of the case. Either the Feminists who seek to make propaganda for their theories out of the misdeeds of the German Army do not know these facts themselves or they are dishonest in their attempt to snatch an advantage out of the war-feeling of the British public. As having had some considerable experience of Germany and things German before the war, I can answer for it that there has been now for years past as strong a current of Feminist sentiment and opinion in Germany as elsewhere, in all circles claiming to be advanced. The only difference is that in Germany, owing to Militarism with its bloodtax, the incidence of which, of course, fell exclusively on men, the injustice of allowing the sex exempted from the blood-tax to swamp with their votes the male elector who was subject to it came home, perhaps, more to the average "man in the street" than in other countries where the same conditions did not prevail. Books on Feminism had a wide circulation. Women had played a part in political agitation for a generation past, at least, in the largest political party in Germany. There was no sex-bar in the matter of membership of that party, or of the share taken in the life of its organization. There was and is, moreover, so far as I am aware, a special organization existing in Germany for the furtherance of female suffrage and other "planks" in the ordinary Feminist programme, while, morebetoken, one of its most prominent leaders is more violent in her jingoism than Count Reventlow himself. All the talk about the position of the German woman, by those who have never lived in Germany, and do not in most cases even know the language, deserves nothing but contempt. It serves the purpose,

222

however, I suppose, of Feminists and advocates of female privilege in general, for pointing a moral and adorning a tale in favour of their own nostrum.

The trick of using a wave of war-hatred and prejudice for the purpose of snatching an advantage is not a new one, and Feminists are not the only offenders. In the present instance the religious bodies are quite equal to trying-on the same game. Just as certain Feminists seek to make out the "frightfulness" of the German Army to be due to the absence of Feminism in Germany, so the Christian sects want to make it out to be due to German lack of "religion" and the influence of "materialism." This in face of the fact that the Kaiser talks more about God than all the prominent military and political personages on the side of the Allies put together, and that the most truculent incitements to national hatred and cruelty have been formulated from the pulpits of German Protestant pastors. They ignore at the same time the circumstance that the majority of the educated as well as the working classes of the French nation are avowedly freethinkers, and yet the French Army has not developed any "frightfulness" as yet, so far as I am aware. Of course, they will say, I suppose, that German religiosity is not of their own true, genuine, and approved brand. This is the usual retort, and one that anybody can make, but the fact remains that you have in Germany all the accredited forms of Christianity represented, Catholic and Protestant, with their services every Sunday, as in other countries. As for the decline in the belief in dogmatic theology, that is not peculiar to Germany, but is common to the whole civilized world.

If I mistake not, the "social purity" mongers have also made an attempt to snatch their bit of advantage by exploiting current anti-Germanism. According to them, of course, the evil mentality from which the German nation is alleged to be suffering at the present time is due to an insufficiently severe standard of sexual manners in their unhappy country. Now, this statement, I do not hesitate to say, speaking in comparison with other countries, has no foundation whatever in fact. Not only is there not a trace of evidence that laxity in sexual behaviour is more prevalent in Germany than among any other European peoples, but, if one comes to that, the Balkan populations, including the Servian and Roumanian, will probably be found on investigation to be farther from the chaste heaven of the "social purist" than any section of the German nation. Besides, it is well known that there was an active "social purity" campaign in Germany before the war, which was not, I believe, the case in (say) France or Italy. I can recall in the Spring of 1914 reading a long report in one of the leading German newspapers of a great "social purity" meeting in Frankfort, in which those enrolling themselves in the league by which the meeting was called were required to take a pledge never under any circumstances to utter a loose jest, or to tell a story that might raise the colour on the most sensitive maiden's cheek! Besides, as regards cruelty, it would not be difficult to show, if one wanted to, that there is a tendency in the "social purity" campaign itself to develop cruelty : witness the flogging clauses of the so-called "White Slave" Act of 1912. No, it is assuredly not the absence of "Feminism" or of "religion," or of "social purity" which is responsible for the aggressive war-mania of Germany, or for the way the war has been conducted by the German Army. It is the ascendancy of Prussia and the Prussian military caste throughout the German-speaking countries of Central Europe, its material power in government, and its moral influence derived therefrom, with its inculcation of war and military glory as the highest aim of the nation – this is the all-sufficient explanation of what has happened. The disingenuous attempts to exploit the situation in the interest of special nostrums are beside the mark and altogether lacking in basis.

In the short sketch contained in the present volume, we have come into contact with many social and intellectual changes, in this country especially, though corresponding changes might easily be traced throughout the civilized world, many of them by no means slight in their character, within the limits of a lifetime, representing at the moment of writing scarcely two generations.

The economic changes that have taken place, considerable though they have been, have not been fundamental. They have been on the line of continuous development, rather than revolutionary in character. The great industry of modern times was already in full swing when I was born. All the main trunk-lines of the English railways have been in existence as long as I can remember. The modern forms of industry, commerce, and finance were already in substance firmly established a generation or two before I was born. Great as has been their development during my lifetime, they are not changed in essentials. The "opening-up" of the outlying, the barbaric, and savage parts of the earth to capitalistic enterprise and exploitation has gone on apace with geographical exploration and discovery. The great capitalistic era has given birth to Socialism as an active faith and ideal with a large section of the working-classes, and with thinking men and sincere well-wishers for Humanity among all classes. The growth of socialistic sympathy among large sections of the population, as well as the formation of a Socialist party that counts in all countries, are events that have evolved themselves since my youth. Of the further development of these factors, or of the appearance above the horizon in the near future of new factors, I refrain from speculating at the present moment. *Qui vivra verra!* – whether I shall be one of those who will see them I know not.

In politics I have seen the aftermath of the '48 movement, and the rise of the new spread-eagleism, the political side of the latter-day developments of Capitalism, with the race of modern armaments which has issued in the present World War. I have witnessed the growth of this upas-tree of modern Imperialism in all civilized countries-the rush for new markets and for new populations to force under the yoke of wage-slavery, and all under cover of the hypocritical "swindle" of Patriotism, the "white man's burden," and so forth. At the same time I have witnessed the birth and growth among the various nations of the tender plant of Internationalism, and have done my little to promote it; and although for the moment beaten down by the winds of national hatred and passion, I am more convinced than ever that before another two or three generations are passed it will have grown to be a mighty tree, while the principles opposed to it will be withering beneath its shade, as the ideal of national *independence* will largely have given way before that of national *interdependence*.

In Philosophy, when I began my studies the British empiricists and the Scottish Psychologists held the field. Mill, Bain, and Lewes, on the one side, and Hamilton and Mansel on the other, were in their glory. But the great English philosopher of the seventies and eighties was Herbert Spencer, whose "synthetic philosophy" was regarded as the last word of speculative wisdom. By way of reaction there is now, of course, a tendency unduly to depreciate Spencer. This period was followed by the rise of the young Hegelian school at Oxford, partly influenced by a book published some years before, Hutchison Stirling's **Secret of Hegel**, This movement, which ran on for many years, met with its reaction at the opening of the twentieth century, in the shape of various counter-currents, such as Pragmatism at Oxford, and the Philosophy of Henri Bergson, in which the Concept is discredited, and Sense and Immediate Consciousness as the content of Time take the place of the Absolute. The late Professor Sidgwick is reported to have said on one occasion, shortly before his death: "One of the things I could never understand is the relation of the Absolute to Time." This difficulty of interpreting to oneself the inner meaning and significance of Time as regards the Absolute I confess to having felt, and hence can sympathize with. Bergson cuts the knot, if I understand him rightly, in identifying Time with the Absolute *sans phrase*.

But perhaps the most remarkable, and in the true sense of the word epoch-making, change which has taken place within the experience of my lifetime has been the outlook opened up to civilized mankind at large by the doctrine of Evolution. When I was born the notion of Evolution was the dream of a few isolated thinkers. Now it is the basis of Civilized Man's conception of the Universe. This stupendous revolution in the intellectual outlook is comparable, *mutatis mutandis*, with the revolution in material things consequent on the transformation of the conditions of human life wrought by the introduction of the machine industry and the new methods of locomotion in the early part of the nineteenth century. The intellectual world, before and after the acceptance of the doctrine of Evolution, is in its own way analogous to the material world before and after the introduction of machinery, so far as regards the chasm that divides the two epochs from one another – in other words, that separates the world of to-day from all previous periods of human history. The changes I have witnessed in the fifty-odd years which these reminiscences cover, as regards speculative thought, religious sentiment, and toleration of opinion in the British people, are sufficiently dealt with in previous chapters of this book.

When one considers the fragment of the course of history through which one has lived, with its passing show, and the queer personalities that have come and gone while it lasted, the usual reflexions on the evanescence of human interests and concerns crowd in upon us.

> They say the Lion and the Lizard keep
> The Courts where jamshyd gloried and drank deep
> And Bahram, that great Hunter – the Wild Ass
> Stamps o'er his Head and he lies fast asleep.

So it is with the transience of our mundane affairs. But as regards the actual scenes of our doings and sufferings through life, "Old Khayyam" at least had the prospect of his "wilderness," which he found "Paradise enow," remaining after his death as it was in his life, while we, living in the great capitalistic era, have

227

to see the "wildernesses" and "paradises" of our youth become the emplacement of slums or factories even before we die. I, for my part, should not mind the lion and the lizard disporting themselves on the sites of my youthful or mature relaxations, but I must confess I do resent the thought of the railway company keeping them in a metamorphosed condition as shunting yards. I would certainly much rather think that the lion and the lizard keep the Halls where I had "gloried and drunk deep" (not that I ever did so), than that their sites should be reserved, not for the roar of the lion, but for the shriek of the steam whistle. Such is sentiment!

The interest and utility for future ages of the class of literature of which the present work may be taken as a humble and imperfect example have never as yet been fully recognized. The historian, who has made it his task to resuscitate for his contemporaries a period of the past, can never have too much contemporary material of this kind at his disposal. In some respects, the less brilliantly original the writer is, provided he is but a fairly keen observer and gifted with average powers of generalization, the more valuable are his notes and comments. Of this fact **Pepys' Diary** is a crucial illustration. Pepys was by no means a man of genius, but his **Diary** has justly become a classic, as affording us an insight into the real life lived in England in the second half of the seventeenth century, such as we have for few other periods. What would the modem classical scholar not give to have such an imperfect set of reminiscences and reflexions even as those contained in the foregoing pages, written in the year 116 by an inhabitant (say) of Rome, Alexandria, or Antioch, born in the year 54. How many points would be made clear concerning that interesting period of the world's history, which are hopelessly obscure to us now. It would not be amiss if, say, in some family where the literary faculty were not wholly lacking, it should be regarded as a sacred duty for one member of the family, at least, in every generation, on reaching sixty years of age, to pen, for better or for worse, his own account of the times he had lived through. Such a series of autobiographical sketches succeeding each other in a continuous chain of varying literary or intellectual merit, some clever, some commonplace, or even stupid, would be an aid in the distant future to the appreciation of past history which would be simply priceless, as compared with anything the present-day historian has at his disposal for his investigations into the historical period he may be at work upon. If but one person in every generation, before passing into the eternal silences, would leave as a legacy to future mankind a systematic sketch of the inner life of the world and his relations to it, for the fifty or sixty years that his experience covers, he would be performing a real, and, as far as it went, inestimable service to the understanding of human psychology in its historical development, and to laying the foundations of a scientific theory of history.

## Notes

1. I must ask the reader to excuse these concluding reflexions being somewhat varied. Their connexion one with another consists mainly in their reference to the present time and its contrast to former periods within my personal experience.

2. It is a noteworthy fact that the physical degeneration of the Scotchman of to-day is coincident with an increasing abstemiousness as regards whisky. There was, I believe, a Royal Commission established to inquire into the causes of Scottish degeneracy before the war, and, so far as I am aware, no report has as yet been made. It is not probable, however, that in the present anti-alcoholic state of public opinion emphasis would be laid by any Royal Commission on these facts, still less any correlation be admitted between them.